Manipulation Techniques

How To Use Empath Psychology For Reading People Mind. Practical Persuasion Skills, Accelerate Learning To Analyze Human Behavior. Practice Nlp And Dark Psychology.

Table of Contents

Introduction

Using manipulation to control the mind of another person is powerful and fascinating. Since the mind is the key to everything a human being does, the ability to control that mind gives multitudes of power and ability. Techniques used to control the mind work because they take control of the thoughts a person has.

Manipulation is about self-awareness, self-management, and relationship management. It's about understanding yourself and having the ability to manage your emotions, plus your response to those emotions.

However, although Dark Psychology can be learned, it isn't something you learn in a weekend program and be "covered" for the others of your life. That is a lifelong learning skill that needs to be practiced and improved on throughout life.

To consider yourself emotionally intelligent, you should try to build up empathy which can make it easy to connect with others and know how they feel. Empathetic people are those people who are genuinely thinking about others and who readily offer support and help to those who require it. Not everyone can place themselves in other folks' shoes and try to understand their motives, which explain why empathy can be such a very important skill.

For this very reason, developing Dark Psychology should come easily to a person who is a natural empath or a people person. Others can find out about it in a course or from a created book, but as with most other abilities, to be proficient at it, you need to practice and apply emotional intelligence to as much situations as possible.

However, having high empathy is not easy. You need to be willing to listen in to various other person's feelings and attitude, to try and understand their behavior, to pay attention without judgment, etc. Not everyone can do this, which explains why many believe that empathy is not a skill, but a natural gift.

In other words, Dark Psychology people are not empathic only once it suits them, but all the time. This is probably why there are very few extremely empathic people around, although it's no secret that empathy could be faked, either to influence somebody or for self-promotion.

Manipulation has come to carry a negative meaning but that is not necessarily true in all cases. Manipulation merely means to shape or mold something to a new, more desirable shape. Snow can be manipulated into the shape of a snowman. Clay can be manipulated into almost any shape. Small children being taught to take turns when playing and to use their manners are, in a sense, being manipulated by their parents. So manipulation is not always a negative event.

Using manipulation to control the mind of another person is powerful and fascinating. Since the mind is the key to everything a human being does, the ability to control that mind gives multitudes of power and ability. Techniques used to control the mind work because they take control of the thoughts a person has. These techniques are based primarily on the method of Neuro-Linguistic Programming (NLP). Using NLP makes it possible to control other people's minds using specific patterns and strategies.

Chapter 1 What Is Empathy

To absolutely understand the Empath we first begin with the Empathy, because Empathy provides the basics signs and symptoms which an Empath possessed and experience whole life.

Empathy

The English phrase Empathy is derived from the historical Greek word ἐμπάθεια (Empatheia, that means "bodily affection or passion"). It, in effect, stems from both (en, "out, at") and (pathos, "ardor" and "suffering") respectively.

Alexithymia is a word used to explain a deficiency in expertise, processing or describing feelings in oneself, in preference to others. This time period comes from the mixture of two historic Greek phrases: ἀλέξω (alekso, that means "push away, repel, or protect") and θυμός (thymos, which means " The heart, the center of conscience, thinking and awareness. "As a result, alexithymia" push away the emotions.

Empathy, derived from the Greek word Empatheia, this means that "ardor or country of emotion", is the ability to feel what others are feeling. It's extremely a crucial part of human interaction that is regrettably missing in some human beings.

While that lack is extreme, intense problems may be the end result. Empathy is the ability to share or understand other people's feelings. It is far from being a multi-component group, each of which is connected with its own brain family. There are 3 ways of looking at Empathy.

Some other manner to recognize Empathy is to differentiate it from other related constructs. As an example, Empathy entails self-cognizance, as well as the difference between the self and the opposite. In that feel, it's far specific from mimicry, or imitation.

Many animals may display signs of mimicry or emotional contagion to every other animal in ache. However, without a few levels of self-awareness, and difference among the self and the opposite, it is not Empathy in a strict feel. Empathy is likewise extraordinary from sympathy, which entails feeling a problem for the struggling of some other man or woman and a choice to help.

That stated, Empathy isn't always a completely unique human enjoy. It's been observed in many non-human primates and even rats.

People frequently say psychopaths lack Empathy but this isn't continually the case. In fact, Psychopathy is enabled by the right cognitive Empathic skills - you need to apprehend what your sufferer is feeling when you are torturing them. What psychopaths generally lack is sympathy. They recognize the opposite character is suffering however they simply don't care.

Studies have additionally shown people with psychopathic tendencies are frequently excellent at regulating their emotions.

Types Of Empathy

There also are, but, unique kinds of Empathy that have been defined via psychologists. Those are cognitive, emotional and compassionate Empathy

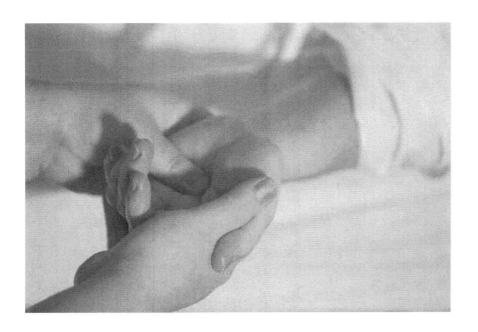

Cognitive Empathy

It's far a beneficial ability, especially in negotiations for instance, or for managers. It permits you to put yourself in someone else's footwear, but without necessarily engaging with their feelings. It does no longer, however, actually match with the definition of Empathy as 'feeling with', being a much greater rational and logical technique.

Efficiently, cognitive Empathy is 'Empathy through thought', rather than with the aid of feeling.

Emotional Empathy

Emotional Empathy is whilst you quite actually experience the opposite person's feelings alongside them, as in case you had 'stuck' the emotions.

Emotional Empathy is likewise called 'non-public misery' or 'emotional contagion'. This is closer to the same old knowledge of the phrase 'Empathy', however greater emotional.

Emotional Empathy might be the first kind of Empathy that many people feel as youngsters. It can be visible when a mother smiles at her infant, and the child 'catches' her emotion and smiles returned. Less fortunately, possibly, a baby will frequently begin to cry if she or he hears every other toddler crying.

Emotional Empathy Can Be Both Good And Bad

Emotional Empathy is right as it method that we can conveniently apprehend and feel other humans' feelings. This is essential for those in caring professions, including docs and nurses, on the way to respond to their sufferers correctly. It is also way that we will reply to friends and others when they are distressed.

Emotional Empathy is terrible, because it's extremely possible to grow to be overwhelmed by way of those emotions, and therefore unable to reply. That is known as Empathy overload and is defined in greater element in our web page on understanding others. Properly strength will help doctors and nurses to keep away from viable burnout from Empathizing too much. There may be a threat, however, that they can turn out to be 'hardened' and now not respond correctly. There were several latest cases in the UK, which include in South Staffordshire, in which nurses and others had been accused of being uncaring. This may be a probable result of over-protection against Empathy overload.

Compassionate Empathy

Sooner or later, compassionate Empathy is what we commonly apprehend with the aid of Empathy: feeling a person's pain, and taking movement to assist.

The call, compassionate Empathy, is constant with what we typically apprehend by using compassion. Like sympathy, compassion is a ready feeling difficulty for someone, however with an additional flow closer to movement to mitigate the trouble.

Compassionate Empathy in the form of Empathy is usually maximum suitable.

As a standard rule, folks who want or need your Empathy don't just need you to apprehend (cognitive Empathy), and that they simply don't need you just to experience their ache or, worse with the emotional Empathy.

Instead, they want you to apprehend and sympathize with what they may be going via and, crucially, either take or help them to take, action to resolve the problem, that's compassionate Empathy.

We can find the right balance between logic and emotion by exercising compassionate Empathy.

We can sense some other man or woman's pain, as if it turned into going on to us and consequently explicit the precise quantity of sympathy.

At the same time, we can also stay on top of things of our personal emotions, and practice purpose to the situation.

This means we can make higher selections and provide the appropriate assistance to them when and wherein it is essential.

Searching For Balance

Also, intellectual compassion can be viewed as under-emotional.

It involves inadequate feeling, and consequently possibly an excessive amount of logical analysis. It is able to be perceived as an unsympathetic response by using the ones in misery.

Emotional Empathy Is Over-Emotional.

Too much emotion or feeling can be unhelpful. As our web page on handling feelings explains, emotions are very primitive. It is very tough to help all people else in case you are overcome with the aid of your personal feelings.

On occasion, easy instinct isn't what you're feeling. You could sincerely be an emotional Empath.

It's k to be emotional. In truth, feeling sturdy emotions has many exact factors. Unluckily, being around terrible humans may have the reverse effect. If so, it can be draining.

To be an emotional Empath takes electricity. In spite of everything, Empathy allows you to take in emotions from all around you, even feelings you don't recognize. It is able to even be overwhelming looking to type out all the emotional airwaves.

You sense overrun by using emotion in case you're an Empath – an emotional processor.

Some Other Types Of Empathy

For finishing touch, it is worth citing that a few human beings suggest that there are two other varieties of Empathy, somatic and religious.

Somatic Empathy

As an instance, in case you see person harm, you too may feel the bodily ache. Anecdotally, equal twins now and again document that they recognize when the opposite has been hurt, which might be an instance of somatic Empathy. You can see an echo of somatic Empathy, as an instance, if someone is hit within the stomach with a ball at some point in a sports activities game, and one or two of the spectators may double over as though they too were hit.

Spiritual Empathy

Spiritual Empathy is defined as a direct connection with a 'higher being' or consciousness.

How Is Empathy Measured?

Those usually ask humans to signify how plenty they trust statements those degree one-of-a-kind varieties of Empathy.

The QCAE, as an example, has statements which include, "It affects me very a lot whilst one in all my friends is upset", that's a degree of affective Empathy.

Cognitive Empathy is determined by using the QCAE via setting fees on a statement such as, "I try to observe all and sundry's facet of a disagreement before I make a decision."

The use of the QCAE, we these days found folks who rating better on affective Empathy have greater gray remember, which a group of various types of nerve cells is, the fore Insula is called in a place of the brain.

This vicinity is regularly involved in regulating positive and negative feelings through integrating environmental stimulants – along with seeing a vehicle coincidence - with visceral and automatic physical sensations.

We additionally determined individuals who rating better on cognitive Empathy had greater grey be counted in the dorsomedial prefrontal cortex.

This place is normally activated all through more cognitive processes, such as the idea of mind that is the potential to attribute intellectual ideals to yourself and any other character. It additionally involves understanding that others have beliefs, goals, intentions, and perspectives exclusive from one's own.

Empathy Be Selective

Research indicates we generally experience more Empathy for members of our very own organization, inclusive of the ones from our ethnic group. As an instance, one look at scanned the brains of Chinese language and Caucasian contributors at the same time as they watched motion pictures of contributors to their personal ethnic institution in pain. In addition, they found people from a unique ethnic organization in pain.

The researchers found that a brain area called the anterior cingulated cortex, that's often active when we see others in ache, changed into much less active when participants noticed individuals of ethnic organizations specific from their personal in ache.

Other studies have discovered brain regions worried in Empathy are less lively when watching human beings in ache who act unfairly. We even see activation in mind areas worried in subjective satisfaction, such as the ventral striatum, while watching a rival game team fail.

But, we do not constantly sense less Empathy for folks who aren't individuals of our very own institution. In our recent examine, students had to deliver economic rewards or painful electric shocks to students from the same or a distinctive university. We scanned their brain responses whilst this took place.

Mind areas involved in worthwhile others have been more lively when human beings rewarded participants of their personal group, however regions involved in harming others have been equally energetic for each corporation.

These effects correspond to observations in daily lifestyles. We usually sense happier if our own institution individuals win something, but we're not going to damage others just due to the fact they belong to a one of a kind institution, lifestyle or race. In well-known, in group bias is more about in-group love in preference to exposed group hate.

But in a few conditions, it may be helpful to experience much less Empathy for a specific group of humans. As an instance, in conflict, it might be useful to feel less Empathy for human beings you are attempting to kill, specifically if they are also looking to damage you.

At the same time as watching the films, human beings had to pretend they were killing actual people. We discovered the lateral orbit frontal cortex, generally lively when people harm others, changed into lively whilst people shot innocent civilians.

The more guilt individuals felt about taking pictures of civilians, the greater the response to this place.

But, the equal region turned into not activated while human beings shot the soldier that was looking to kill them.

The consequences provide insight into how people regulate their feelings. In addition they display the brain mechanisms commonly implicated while harming others become less active when the violence against a selected organization is seen as justified.

This might offer future insights into how human beings turn out to be desensitized to violence or why a few humans feel more or much less guilty about harming others.

Our Empathetic brain has advanced to be extraordinarily adaptive to distinctive forms of conditions. Having Empathy may be very useful because it often enables us to recognize others so we will assist or mislead them, however occasionally we need a good way to transfer of our Empathetic feelings to guard our personal lives, and people of others.

Need Of Empathy

Empathy is essential because it allows us to understand how others are feeling so we will respond appropriately to the scenario. It's far normally related to social behavior and there is a lot of studies showing that more Empathy leads to more helping behavior.

But, this is not always the case. Empathy also can inhibit social movements or even lead to amoral behavior. For instance, a person who sees a car accident and is crushed by using emotions witnessing the victim in excessive pain might be less probable to help that man or woman.

Further, robust Empathetic feelings for contributors of our own family or our own social or racial group might result in hate or aggression towards those we understand as a danger. Think about a parent defensive their infant or a nationalist defensive their United States of America.

The psychopath may choose to push the person off the bridge more often than not. It reflects the pragmatic theory which provides an excellent element of protecting 5 people's lifestyles by using murdering one man or woman. So one ought to argue people with psychopathic tendencies are extra moral than normal human beings – who in all likelihood wouldn't push the man or woman off the bridge – as they're much less motivated by using feelings when making ethical selections.

Chapter 2 How Empathy Impacts In People's Lives

Heading out into society in this day and age can be quite daunting. It is said that there are two types of societies. We will take a look at each, then see how they intertwine with each other.

Community

A communal society is one that everyone benefits from — meaning, there is a balance between what an individual wants and what is best for the community. The community is always the primary recipient in order to maintain peace, harmony, and balance. When there is a communal society, the people within it tend to put their own wants and needs aside for the greater good of that community. The community members are put second in comparison to the community as a whole. Thus, when the community is suffering, the individuals within suffer as well. On the other hand, if the community does well and has many benefits, the individuals in that community will benefit from it as well. Some people may not like that idea because there may be some people who work extremely hard for the community, but there are others who do not lift a finger. This may be difficult for some to handle because everyone will get the same benefits regardless of how much work one does. In order for this to work, everyone needs to be on board.

Individual

In this society, people are able to focus on their own success, identities, and skills. The community as a whole will not be the focus, nor will they have any issues if the individual fails or does not become as successful as they thought. An individual-oriented society will allow individuals to focus on their own goals. This type of society is about the personal development and achievement of each individual. The focus here is not on the peace and well-being of the entire community but the happiness of each individual. Let's just think about a society where someone is wildly successful. They typically end up giving back to the community where they grew up or lived in; thus, the community benefits from the individual's success as well.

Some people actually have a mixture of both societies. When they are both intertwined with each other, it can be difficult to focus on what is better for which. It happens when a person lives in an individualistic mindset but also has empathy toward others. It can be somewhat of a battle if someone has these two ideals intertwined. For example, they want to succeed, but they also want to help everyone else out. Many people who have this internal conflict tend to get anxiety, depression, and/or have low self-esteem. There are many factors to consider when someone is searching for the reason why they isolate themselves. They may feel as if they are unworthy of love or success. They may be depressed, or they may have a combination of all due to low self-esteem. There are plenty of factors, both environmental and societal, that are contributing, along with trauma and past abuse. It is important to recognize and be aware of the different issues that people face when trying to help themselves as well as others.

Since empaths do have both individual and communal goals, it can be hard for them to find their place in society that is satisfying for both aspects.

Social Anxiety and Empaths

Being an empath can be tough, especially when you are expected at social functions of all sorts. Social anxiety is typically common with empaths; however, some may just be describing the feelings that they get when they are around others that are quite toxic. We have to remember that we are all human beings, and we do need a human connection with others. When someone explains and states that they have social anxiety, they may be seen as odd or weird in some way. However, social anxiety does not mean we have something wrong with our character. It may actually indicate that we may be more intelligent. Anxiety puts us on high alert. Those who are mothers and have children typically have more anxiety than others. They want to protect their children, hence why they develop a sense of heightened awareness.

There are five signs that your social anxiety may be an empath sensitivity:

1. It is selective.
2. You were not bullied or abused in childhood.
3. You do not fear rejection; rather, you avoid people who make you uncomfortable.
4. You are a pro at reading people.
5. Crowded places make you feel overwhelmed.

It is selective. If you are just fine at times but tend to become extremely anxious when around certain people, then your anxiety is selective. When you come across some with low vibes, you may tend to heighten your senses, which can be quite overwhelming. This could be when someone makes you uncomfortable. You can typically tell if they have hidden bad feelings toward you, if they have negative emotions, or if they are being passive-aggressive. You will start to notice people's body language when you are around, and you will begin to understand your surroundings, plus the way you may react to it. If you do find that being around someone in particular gives you intense anxiety, try to figure out what it might be about them that is causing this. It could be your gut telling you to get away from that person as they mean harm to you. Just try to be aware of your body and mind when you are in any situation that makes you anxious.

You were not bullied or abused in childhood. Typically, when someone has anxiety, it stems from a traumatic event in childhood, such as being bullied or abused. However, if you did not have any of that happen to you, you may just be able to pick up on other people's vibrations.

You do not fear rejection; rather, you avoid people who make you uncomfortable. It has been said that social anxiety is tied to an overwhelming fear of being rejected. It could be that you are afraid of being laughed at or not fitting in. However, what if you do not have a fear of rejection? It might not actually be that you fear rejection; it could be that you are afraid of other people due to the bad energy that they give off. That bad energy may drain you, so you might not want to be around them. Fear can be tricky at times. You can say that you may be afraid of someone, but understanding why and then taking action to avoid them will be the best for your health. In this instance, it is not about the fear of rejection; it is about your dislike for the way that certain people make you feel uncomfortable.

You are a pro at reading people. If there is ever a time when you get a gut feeling when you are in a situation and just cannot put your finger on what it may mean, it may be that you are picking up on someone's ill intent or toxic existence in your presence. If you are repulsed by someone the first time you meet them, then you could be sensing that they have low morals or standards. They could take advantage of you or could potentially harm you in some way. This instinct happens because empaths can sense nuances in behaviors, such as nonverbal cues or body language (e.g., not looking in the eye). These cues will tell the empath when someone is lying to them and will let them sense when someone is up to something that is not authentic. If someone is being inauthentic, lying, or hiding something, you will be able to pick up on that. Always listen to your gut.

Crowded places make you feel overwhelmed. Crowded spaces can be a huge drain of energy for an empath. Thus, you tend to feel depleted when you are surrounded by too many different energies. If you tend to avoid places that are particularly busy during peak hours, such as a grocery store or a mall, because you know it drains the energy from you, you are considered an energy-sensitive empath. There are also ways that this causes physical issues, such as dizziness and weakness. So if you find yourself with any physical or emotional symptoms while in crowded spaces, it is time to choose your outings wisely in order to save your own energy.

Social anxiety can be seen as a way for empaths to hold close the true connections that they currently have with others, and it is not that they cannot form new connections. Having social anxiety is not necessarily a bad thing, even though people may treat you like it is. When your brain is always active, you are constantly searching and analyzing your surroundings. It is said to be a protection tool, and that, to most, is never a bad thing.

So what if you do not like how social anxiety tends to take over your life? How does one prevent this from happening? Here are some tips on how to prevent empaths from developing anxiety:

1. Mix it up.
2. Express emotions.
3. Talk to your emotions.
4. Clear your inner self.
5. Ask for help.

Mix it up. If you keep your feelings bottled up, you will end up feeling quite anxious, and that could lead to depression. However, expressing your emotions will allow you to feel a sense of clarity. Keep yourself busy so your mind does not dwell on certain situations and issues. If you are not busy or cannot mix up your schedule, try to find someone to confide in that you trust. If you are able to get your feelings out, they will not stay bottled up inside.

Express emotions. The more you repress your emotions, the more likely you will have an end result of depression. One way to do this is to practice catharsis. Catharsis is something that can be provoked or happen naturally, such as when you are laughing or crying. Some people find it best to relax in a bath, where it is just you and your emotions to release in a private space.

Talk to your emotions. In order to understand your emotions, you must know yourself. If you are not emotional literate, how you can relate to your feelings, then you will not experience any personal development. When you are in tune with your own feelings, you tend to understand yourself on a higher level. Plus, when you question your own emotions and thoughts to self-reflect, you will find that you are more calm and relaxed.

Clear your inner self. We have to pay attention to how the world around us may have an impact on our own consciousness. Some people may want to start by cleaning their private space as soon as they wake up. It will seem that, as you are cleaning your personal space, you are also keeping a clear mind to start your day.

Ask for help. Most empaths do not want to burden anyone else, so they do hesitate to ask others for help. If calling your friends to vent to them is a way to relieve your stress, then find a friend who does not mind that you do that. If they are a true friend to you, they will recognize when you need the most help.

Just try not to interpret or assume anyone else's emotions. Try to block them out instead of bottling them in and worrying. Worrying will only turn into anxiety, and anxiety is not good for your overall mental and physical health. Use the five tips above. If you try one and it does not work for you, try another. Figure out what works best for you and use that to the fullest in order to combat any anxiety that may have been coming your way.

Chapter 3 Mind Control Tactics

Mind control involves using influence and persuasion to change the behaviors and beliefs in someone. That someone might be the person themselves or it might be someone else. Mind control has also been referred to as brainwashing, thought reform, coercive persuasion, mental control, and manipulation, just to name a few. Some people feel that everything is done by manipulation. But if that is true to be believed, then important points about manipulation will be lost. Influence is much better thought of as a mental continuum with two extremes. One side has influences that are respectful and ethical and work to improve the individual while showing respect for them and their basic human rights. The other side contains influences that are dark and destructive that work to remove basic human rights from a person, such as independence, the ability for rational thought, and sometimes their total identity.

When thinking of mind control, it is better to see it as a way to use influence on other people that will disrupt something in them, like their way of thinking or living. Influence works on the very basis of what makes people human, such as their behaviors, beliefs, and values. It can disrupt the very way they chose personal preferences or make critical decisions. Mind control is nothing more than using words and ideas to convince someone to say or do something they might never have thought of saying or doing on their own.

There are scientifically proven methods that can be used to influence other people. Mind control has nothing to do with fakery, ancient arts, or even magical powers. Real mind control really is the basis of a word that many people hate to hear. That word is marketing. Many people hate to hear that word because of the negative connotations associated with it. When people hear "marketing," they automatically assume that it refers to those ideas taught in business school. But the basis of marketing is not about deciding which part of the market to target or deciding which customers will likely buy this product. The basis of marketing is one very simple word. That word is "YES."

If a salesperson asks a regular customer to write a brief endorsement of the product they buy, hopefully, they will say yes. If someone asks their significant other to take some of the business cards to pass out at work, hopefully, they will say yes. If you write any kind of blog and ask another blogger to provide a link to yours on their blog, hopefully, they will say yes. When enough people say yes, the business or blog will begin to grow. With even more yesses, it will continue to grow and thrive. This is the very simple basis of marketing. Marketing is nothing more than using mind control to get other people to buy something or to do something beneficial for someone else. And the techniques can easily be learned.

The first technique in mind control is to tell people what you want them to want. Never tell people to think it over or take some time. That is a definite mind control killer. People already have too much going on in their minds. When they are told to think something over they will not. It will be forgotten, and then it will never happen. This has nothing to do with being stupid or lazy and everything to do with just being way too busy.

So the best strategy is to take the offensive and think for them. Everything must be explained in the beginning. Never assume that the other blogger will automatically understand the benefits of adding a link will be for them. Do not expect anyone to give a demonstration blindly. And merely asking for a testimonial, while it might garner an appositive response, probably will not garner a well-formed testimonial to the product. Instead, be prepared to explain the blog, show examples, and offer compelling reasons why this merger will be a benefit to both parties. Have the demonstration laid out in great detail with notes on what to say when and visuals to go along with the notes, so all the other person has to do is present the information. Offer the customer a few variations of testimonials that have already been received and ask them to choose one and personalize it a bit. Always be specific in explaining what is desired. Explain why it is desired. Show how this will work. Tell the person how to do it and why they should do it. If done correctly it will feel exactly like one friend advising another friend on which is the best path to take. And the answer will be yes simply because saying yes makes so much sense.

Think of the avalanche. Think of climbing all the way to the top of the highest mountain ever. Now, at the top, think of searching for the biggest heaviest boulder that exists on the mountain. Now, picture summoning up superhuman strength to push this boulder, dislodging it from the place it has rested for years and years. Once this boulder is loosened, it rolls easily over the edge of the cliff, crashing into thousands of other boulders on its way down the mountain, taking half of the mountain with it in a beautiful cascade of rocks and dirt. Imagine sitting there smiling cheerfully at the avalanche that was just created.

Marketing and mind control are very like creating an avalanche. Getting the first person to answer yes might be difficult. But each subsequent yes will be easier and easier. And always start at the top, never the bottom. Starting at the top is definitely more difficult, and it is more likely to come with more negative responses than positive responses in the beginning. But starting at the top also yields a much greater reward when the avalanche does begin. And the results will be far greater than beginning at the bottom of the mountain. Yes, the small rock is easier to push over. Then it can be built upon by pushing over another small rock, then another. This way can work, but it will take much longer than being successful at the top. No one ever went fishing for the smallest fish in the pond or auditioned for the secondary role just to be safe. Everyone wants that top prize. Do not be afraid to go for it.

On the other hand, never ask for the whole boulder the first time. Ask for part of it. This may seem directly contradictory but it is not. Always start with a small piece. Make the beginning easier for everyone to see. Let other people use their own insight to see the end result. When the first bit goes well, then gradually ask for more and more and more.

Think of writing a guest spot for someone else who has their own blog. By sending in the entire manuscript first, there is a greater risk of rejection. Begin small. Send them a paragraph or two discussing them the idea. Then make an outline of the idea and send that in an email. Then write the complete draft you would like them too use and send it along. When asking a customer for a testimonial, start by asking for a few lines in an email. Then ask the customer to expand those few lines into a testimonial that covers at least half a typed page. Soon the customer will be ready for an hour-long webcast extolling the virtues of the product and your great customer service skills.

Everything must have a deadline that really exists. The important word here is the word 'real'. Everyone has heard the salesperson who said to decide quickly because the deal might not be available later or another customer was coming in and they might get it. That is a total fabrication and everyone knows it to be true. There are no impending other customers and the deal is not going to disappear. There is no real sense of urgency involved. But everyone does it. There are too many situations where people are given a totally fake deadline by someone who thinks it will instill a great sense of urgency for completion of the task. It is not only totally not effective but completely unneeded. It is a simple matter to create true urgency.

Only leave free things available for a finite amount of time. When asking customers for testimonials be certain to mention the last possible day for it to be received to be able to be used. Some people will be unable to assist, but having people unable to participate is better than never being able to begin.

Always give before you receive. And do not ever think that giving is fifty-fifty. Always give much more than is expected in return. Before asking for a testimonial from a satisfied customer, be sure to make numerous acts of exceptional customer service. Before asking a blog writer for a link, link theirs to yours many times. This is not about helping someone out so they will help you. This is all about being so totally generous that the person who is asked for the favor cannot possibly say no. It might mean extra work, but that is how to influence other people.

Always stand up for something that is much bigger than average. Do not just write another blog on how to do something. Use an important issue to take a stand and defend the stance with unbeatable logic and fervent passion. Do not just write a how-to manual. Choose a particular idea and sell people on it, using examples of other people with the same idea living the philosophy.

Never feel shame. This does not mean being extremely extroverted to the point of silliness or having a total lack of conscience in business dealings. In the case of mind control shamelessness refers to a total complete belief that this course of action is the best possible course and everyone will benefit greatly from it. This is about writing the best possible blog ever and believing that everyone needs to read it to be able to improve their lives. It is about believing in a particular product so deeply that the feeling is that everyone will benefit from using it. It is knowing deep inside that this belief is the most correct belief ever and everyone should believe it.

Mind control uses the idea that someone's decisions and emotions can be controlled using psychological means. It is using powers of negotiation or mental influence to ensure the outcome of the interaction is more favorable to one person over the other. This is basically what marketing is: convincing someone to do something particular or buy something in particular. Being able to control someone else's mind merely means understanding the power of human emotion and being able to play upon those emotions. It is easier to have a mental impact on people if there is a basic understanding of human emotions. Angry people will back down when the subject of their anger is not afraid. Angry people feed upon the fear of others. Guilt is another great motivator. Making someone feel guilty for not thinking or feeling, in the same manner, is a wonderful way to get them to give in. Another way to use mind control over someone is to point out how valuable they are to the situation. Controlling the mind of another does not mean depriving them of free will and conscious thought.

Chapter 4 Methods Of Persuasion

For some people, the art of persuasion comes easily. You can watch them talk to almost anyone, and it seems like they will always get the response that they want from the other person. On the other hand, there are those people who may have the best message in the world who couldn't convince anyone, even their closest friends, to do something. No matter where you fall in either of these groups though, with a little bit of practice and hard work, you will be able to learn how to use persuasion to your advantage.

In terms of the process of using persuasion, there will usually be three parts that you need to follow including:

The communicator, or the medium used as the source of persuasion

The persuasive nature of the appeal

The audience or the target person that the appeal is going to be sent too.

Each of these elements needs to be accounted for before you try to use persuasion on a higher level. It is always a good practice to look around you and check to see how many instances of persuasion are going on in your daily life. Some of these are going to be overt, but many of them are going to be pretty subtle. This can be great training for persuasion because you will be able to employ the same kind of tactics. Let's take a look at some of the options that you can use when it comes to good persuasion and using the right techniques.

Using the Aristotelian appeals

So, the first option that we are going to look at is the Aristotelian appeals. Aristotle is well-known and is actually one of the most famous persuaders of all time. He believed that there were three main ways that a person could approach thing when they were trying to use persuasion to change the opinion of the other person.

Ethos

The first appeal that one could use was ethos, which is going to focus on things such as trust, integrity, and character. This appeal is going to focus on the reputation of the person and some of the things that they may have done in the past, or even how others think about them today. There are many people who value their reputations, and they will work hard to maintain them, especially if the person is in a high office or in the public eye. This is not a bad thing to care about your reputation.

As the persuader, it is fine to show off some character because this shows that you are a human like everyone else and you can even show off some of the flaws that you have. The trick here is that you need to only show off flaws that are pretty small, ones that the target audience will not see as a big deal, but they do need to be large enough that they show that you are still a person who has some good values and even virtues.

You need to be credible as well if you would like to be persuasive. People are much more likely to believe what you are saying if you are seen as a credible person, someone who is seen as an expert in their chosen field. If you would like to get started with persuading other people to act in a specific way, then you need to start cultivating the right impression with good virtues, small flaws, and by showing that you are an expert in your field.

Pathos

The second appeal that you should work on is pathos, which is when you evoke the emotions of the other person. You will want to find some way to excise the other person, to get their interest in some way. This can often be done with storytelling or even by referencing situations where injustices were done at some point. You can add in some ethos to this by condemning these actions and describing how your values fall into the matter.

If you are working on this appeal, it is important to use the right linguistics. Language is going to be your most important tool for getting the emotions involved. A good speaker will always be able to pick out the right words to get their message out there. For example, they know how to use words that will amplify or subdue the situation based on the results that you want to get.

This can be hard to learn in the beginning, especially if you do not consider yourself to be that great of a speaker. But the next time that there is a big pollical debate or speech going on take the time to listen to the words that they are using. This will help you to see how the words can bring out the right emotions that the communicator is looking for.

Logos

And the third appeal that you can use when it comes to persuasion is logos. This is when you are going to use logic, rational explanations, and even evidence to help support your claims. Some people do not respond that well to the emotional side, and they may feel that anyone who is using their values and integrity are only doing so to make a sale. These people are probably going to do the best with logos, being told logical information that they can look up on their own to verify before they make a decision.

This does not mean that you cannot go through and make some changes to the wording and try to convince these people still. You can always bring the most prominent features to light, or if you know the person, at least bring out the features that are going to appeal to them the most. This is not a license to lie to them about the things that you are doing and saying, but it doesn't hurt to show your argument in the best possible light.

Foot in the door

We talked about this one a bit earlier, but it can be one of the most effective persuasion techniques that are out there. This one allows you to ask for a bigger favor after you have already been granted a smaller favor, especially if they are related in some way. You may start off with something that is pretty small, such as just borrowing a cup of sugar from your neighbor. Your neighbor will probably be fine with this because it's not that big of a deal and most people, as long as they have it on hand, will have a cup of sugar to share with you.

Now that you have asked for that cup of sugar, you may take it up a notch. You may then ask if they have some butter and eggs that you can borrow as well. Since they have already lent you some sugar, they figure it is not a big deal to lend you some more things a well. And the persuader can just keep going, perhaps asking if the target would mind baking the whole cake for them in the end.

If the persuader had started out with asking the neighbor to make the cake, it is unlikely that the neighbor would have agreed. The neighbor might say that they are busy or that they really do not know how to make a cake that well. But since the persuader started out with something small, something that would be silly not to help out with, and then slowly built up from there, the neighbor may eventually feel a sense of obligation to get the work done at this point.

This method can be used in many different persuasion circumstances. The trick is to always start out with something small, something that you think the target will be willing to help you out with. Then you will slowly build yourself up until you get to the bigger thing that you would like them to have in the long run. You may have wanted the target to start with the bigger thing, but if you went there first, you would have completely missed out on the sale.

Reversal tagging

Another option that you can use is known as reversal tagging. This is a trick that uses simple and subtle sentence phrasing to get an agreement, or at least compliance, from the target in general. It is going to use two opposing structures inside the sentence, the first part being an affirmative statement and the second one will be a tag question.

The premise here is that you will make the initial statement to open the line of questioning, but you will add on the tag question so that the target has a binary choice for answering. This will help you to reframe the response so that it sounds like they agree with you the whole time.

For example, you may say something like "You like this house, don't you?" to your spouse. There are a few ways that they can choose to respond to this. If they say "Yes, I like this place" you would respond something like "As I thought, you like this place." On the other hand, if they give you a different response, such as "No, I don't like this place," you can simply turn it around and say "As I thought, you don't like this place."

Statements like the one above are designed to have a negative reversal element to them. If you do them in the proper manner, the statement will hide the command because it becomes a rhetorical question because it will first tell the person what they should be thinking, but then it inserts the question that will offer a level of disagreement, even though it implies that the disagreement is not wanted.

The key to this method is to ensure that the first statement is pretty strong because it is going to be the main persuasive component. This kind of technique is also useful when you are trying to convince the other person to take an action on something, rather than just agreeing with you. It is the same principle, but this time you will state out your negative first before taking a long pause and then adding in the tag question. For example, you could say something like "You aren't able to do that.... Are you?" this implies that the person is not able to do something and it is going to evoke them to respond in a way that will prove you wrong.

Reverse psychology

This is something that you have probably heard about in the past because it is a psychological tactic that is often used when you want to get the other person to take an action. However, if you are not good at performing this tactic, it is going to seem pretty obvious, and it will not work the way that you would like it to. This tactic is basically going to get somebody to do what you would like by suggesting that they do the opposite in the beginning. It is going to be the most effective if you can evoke an emotional response because it will stop the person from thinking rationally through their decision.

This is a principle that can work well with those who like to have control, such as rebellious people or those who just like to do the opposite of what they are told to do. It is often called reactance theory, and it will describe the scenario where a person feels like they are losing control of things and they are going to try to grab that control back by doing the exact opposite of what they have been asked, even if it is not their best interest to do so.

Cognitive dissonance

Have you ever been in a situation where you know that something seems a bit off about it, but you cannot figure out why it doesn't feel right? When there isn't something quite right about a situation, it is going o set off some dissonance in the mind and will trigger the person to try to make it all right. People who have OCD will often know this feeling because they will notice when little things are out of the normal.

If you can change things up a little bit, you may be able to convince the other person to act in the way that you would like. They may feel that their reputation is falling a little bit, that they are missing out on something, or so much else. You can then step in to offer them a solution, an easy to way to change things back to normal, and they are more likely to jump right at it.

Counter-attitudinal advocacy

It is pretty common for people to state a view on something, or even to support an opinion, even if that is not something that they really believe themselves. This isn't necessarily that deceptive because the things that people choose to do this with are usually small or they have the best intentions. For example, it is common for someone to tell a little white lie because it will help to protect the feelings of someone else. When this happens, we are attempting to reduce the dissonance that we caused by saying that our actions are still noble.

Whether you think that telling a little white lie or doing something similar is acceptable or that you think honesty is the best option is irrelevant because you can still use this human tendency to your advantage when you are persuading others. This is a common technique to use when it comes to cults or even gangs when they are trying to change the beliefs of others to justify their behavior.

When you are using this as a persuasion principle, you are going to be tied in with what is known as incremental escalating requests. What this one means is that you are going to offer the target with some small rewards so that they are not really going to attribute this new behavior to some changes. Over time though, the effect is going to keep escalating until it reaches a point where they are doing something that is really different compared to where the behavior started.

A good way to practice this is by getting those you know to go along with you on some small points, but these small points need to have an eventual goal of persuasion that you would like to accomplish. These points need to all be small enough that the internal justification for agreeing with you is not that big of a deal and the other person is not going to resist you or have a lot of questions in the process. Over time, if you have done this properly, the beliefs of the other people should change to fit with yours.

Perceived self-interest

If you ask anyone, they often believe that they are generous and pretty caring creatures. No matter how much most people believe this though, as humans we are really a self-serving species. There have been a lot of studies done on this over the years, and it has been proven over and over again. Even altruism is a self-serving act because it does help the grantor to feel good about themselves in the process.

The idea behind this technique is a pretty simple one to work with, but you will be spending your time on perception. If you can convince your target that they are doing something that is in their best interest, whether that is true or not, then the target is much more likely to go along with the whole thing. This can be really apparent when you are trying to persuade someone who is higher up than you.

For example, you may work with your boss, and you can say something like "I see my job as making you more successful." This can help to endear a new employee to their boss because even if you are getting some of the credit along the way, you are showing that the majority of the limelight is going to go to your boss along the way, and their self-interest is really going to like this.

This one is known as disrupt-then-reframe, and it is similar to offer biasing and Russian front. The idea with this one is to put out a statement that is completely far away from the ideals and belief of the target right from the beginning. This is like making an offer to the other person that they are not really likely to accept. After they have rejected your offer, you are going to do a follow up that is more rational, something that your target is more likely to go along with, especially since they are still comparing it to your first offer in their heads. Of course, the second suggestion that you make is usually going to be the one that you wanted to persuade the target to in the first place.

It is similar to reverse tagging, but it is going to include a longer statement. The aim here is to disrupt the other person is thinking and then show them that you can still be rational in the process and that you want to work with them to a better goal. Since you are working with them, and the second request is not so ridiculous compared to the first one that you made, the target is much more likely to go along with what you are suggesting.

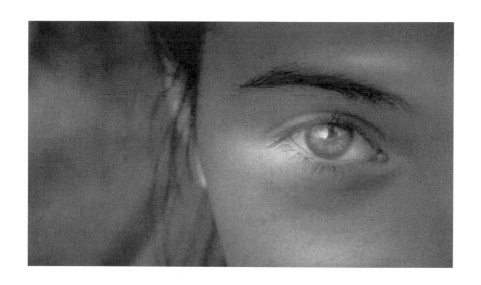

Hurt and rescue principle

This principle is going to be based off evoking some discomfort or fear in the person from the start. When the person is assessing their options for a solution, you will be able to offer the perfect solution in the form of the thing you want to persuade them to. You need to be able to manufacture a level of discomfort here first and being crafty enough to make this work can be hard.

Since you are trying to bring in some fear or discomfort with your target, you do need to be a bit careful with this option. It is not a good idea to come off as aggressive or intimidating in the process because this will just turn the person away from you completely.

For example, you may work with someone and say that you have noticed that their performance has dropped off recently and that there may be an issue with their funding getting cut off because of it. Now that the other person is worried about what is going to happen with their funding and their job, you can come in as the one with a solution. You may say something like you have convinced them to not do that just yet as long as the other person can start meeting their performance metrics again.

Of course, you will need to go through and change things around to work with the thing that you are trying to sell or the thing that you are trying to persuade the other person to do. But the point is that you will start out by adding in some discomfort or fear for the target before providing them with the solution that will make things all better.

Trial ballooning

Another option that you can use is known as trial ballooning or trial closing. This is the starting point, and it is relevant whether you are the seller or the buyer in the negotiation. The idea is to start out with the final solution that you would like to end up. You will just put that information out there and see if the thing works.

With this tactic, there is nothing wrong with going a little bit big right from the beginning. Being the one to make the first offer in this kind of exchange will usually put you in the worst position because you have shown all of your cards and this is why it is so important for you to go as bold as possible. When you start out with an aggressive offer, it will provide the anchor that is needed to help you get a good deal. The other person is going to bring you down from that anchor spot so going high helps you to get closer to your goals.

And you never know, your big offer may not seem so bad to the other person, and they may be willing to just give in right from the beginning. If the other person is really in a hurry to come to a resolution, they will really take this balloon offer, and you will come out ahead.

Auction model

This strategy is a good one to put in place if you are working with more than one buyer at the same time. Otherwise, it is not going to be the best one. With this method, you want to play one of the parties against the others so that there is a buying frenzy and it is more likely that the price is going to be driven up, no matter what you are trying to sell.

It is human nature to be competitive, and when they are faced with some opposition to something that they would like, their primitive instincts are going to come out. Possession seems to be an innate for most of us, especially if we haven't gone through to rationally appraise the real use for the item ahead of time. The persuader will be able to use their advantage, getting all the buyers in the deal to jump on board and try to pay more than the other person.

As you can see, there are a lot of different techniques that you can use when it comes to being successful with persuasion. The one that you will choose often depends on the goals that you have in mind, what you are trying to persuade the other person to do, your comfort level, and how hard the other person will be to persuade. Try a few of them out and see which one works the best for you.

Chapter 5 Persuading and Influencing People Using Manipulation

Human being as a social being is in constant communication for many reasons, giving information, getting information, asking for help, making promises, telling your feelings and thoughts, or trying to learn someone else's feelings and thoughts, and so on. Communication is established within a certain structure and order.

The concept of persuasion is defined in the dictionary as follows: Convincing, convincing; deceit; "Based on this definition, it will not be wrong to consider persuasion as a form of communication that is realized to achieve the desired aims." Indeed, when we look carefully, it can be seen that the difference between daily communication and persuasion is to achieve the desired goal. Not every communication phenomenon that is established in daily life is intended for persuasion, asking someone's memory only aims to learn about the person's condition and health. However, rather than persuading a person on a particular issue, it should be dealt with to uncover the desired change in the person who is exposed in the final analysis, which should be established with a certain systematic structure.

In the meantime, an important issue should be included here. It is also the effects of communication and how they occur. The effects of communication are:

1. Change in the recipient's level of knowledge

2. Changes in the attitude of the recipient

3. A change in the receiver's opens behavior.

In the second stage, the attitude change that came into the agenda is also realized in three ways:

1. Strengthening or strengthening the existing attitude

2. Change of existing attitude

3. New attitude formation

The effects of communication are often expected to occur sequentially and usually do. It is possible to see the effect of communication to a large extent in the change that may occur in open behavior. This is where the difference between daily communication and persuasion comes up. Persuasive communication is the expected and desired changes in attitude and open behavioral changes that will occur after the information is given. The attitude change that is expected to occur is determined by some attitude measurement techniques (Likert scale, etc.) developed in cases where open behavioral change can't be observed clearly or if it's not possible for different reasons, for example, an individual's Facebook, and so on. If it is desired to learn the attitude towards social media, a questionnaire consisting of expressions reflecting this attitude can be prepared. These statements; it allows people to share, enjoy the time, etc. can. It is possible to say that a Likert-type scale was used to measure the attitudes of the respondents to measure attitudes.

The concept and process of persuasion is a subject that has been studied intensively. In general, the biggest factors contributing to the success and failure of communication emerge as convincing communication and its proper structuring. With good understanding and knowledge of persuasive techniques; an educator, an advertiser, or a politician, in other words, it is possible to evaluate anyone whose purpose is to change the thoughts and actions of others. It should not be ignored that some essential variables exist in persuasion. Each of the variables in persuasion must be identifiable, distinguishable, and measurable. Scientists working in this field, these variables fall under two headings. These are called "dependent variables" and "independent variables. Arguments are made or occur with the communication process. We know what these variables will be, how they will be formed, and predict and produce their effects. Dependent variables, on the other hand, have to be done, and convincingly. We often hope to replace dependent variables with independent variables that we manage and control. Dependent and independent variables are called a convincing communication matrix.

The convincing communication matrix is a precise and complete data about all dependent and independent variables in human relationships throughout human life. Independent variables should be considered in many aspects and aspects of communication. However, dependent variables occur only when a person receives a persuasive message in terms of the information process. The main issue that needs to be emphasized about independent variables is the operation of the basic process of communication: "who, whom, what, through which channel and what kind of influences. The arguments that make up every convincing communication state appear in this case as "source, message, channel, receiver, and purpose. The dependent variables of the persuasive communication matrix are divided into six steps according to the characteristics of new behaviors, events, and phenomena in which the person is convinced. First, a convincing message must be presented. The second step is the participation of the target person in the communication, and this person needs to understand what is to be discussed. It's important that the recipient supports communication until the message is sent later and third. The fourth step is the understanding of the message, as well as the acceptance of the recipient or at least verbal adjustment. The fifth step is the most basic requirement. This step is the ability to accept until the effect can be measured. The sixth and last step or dependent variable is the ability of the target person to show the new behavior as open behavior. For example; depending on the main objective of the persuasion campaign, the purchase of a certain product, the selection of the candidate or leaving a harmful habit, etc. they are always concrete indicators of this last dependent variable. An analysis in the context of dependent and independent variables can help organize ideas about persuasion. The persuasion process is analyzed at all levels of communication.

These steps are as follows: Source of communication, form, content, and organization of communication, characteristics of the channel to which the message will be delivered, ability and characteristics of the intended recipient and intended behavior and attitude changes. Thus, under these five headings of communication, the efficiency of the persuasive communication process performed under the six steps of the dependent variables of persuasion is defined and evaluated. Examination of the persuasion process shows the importance of understanding and attention in a way. For example; when asked what kind of connection can be made between an intelligent buyer and persuasion, he will probably tell you that only a much smarter individual can convince that person. In other words, the more knowledgeable and intelligent person can only direct the person's point of view to another party. This point shows the variables of the connection between intelligence and persuasive communication. However, other points that should not be forgotten are the role and importance of attention and acceptance in the persuasion process.

Persuasion Techniques

The basis of persuasion is to direct the other person to the thought you desire and to make it normal in the basic belief and vision system. To simplify, it is to make the other person think the way you want. That's exactly what it means to convince. If the other person thinks the way you want, you can take the action that you want to take, that is, buying a product or consuming a product. Located below are techniques to persuade and convince some of the most effective techniques effectively. Persuasion techniques are not limited to these, but they are important for efficiency. You may encounter many other techniques of persuasion, such as rewarding, punishing, creating a positive or negative perception.

1. Creating Needs

One of the best methods of persuasion is to create a need or to reassure an old need. This question of need is related to self-protection and compatibility with basic emotions such as love. This technique is one of the biggest trumps of marketers in particular. They try to sell their products or services using this technique. The kind of approaches that express the purchase of a product to make one feel safe or loving is part of the need-building technique.

2. Touching Social Needs

The basis of the technique of touching social needs are factors such as being popular, having the prestige, or having the same status as others. The advertisements on television are the ideal examples. People who buy the products in these advertisements think that they will be like the person in the advertisement or they will be as prestigious. The main reason why persuasion techniques such as touching social needs are effective is related to television advertising. Many people watch television for at least 1-2 hours a day and encounter these advertisements.

3. Use of Meaningful and Positive Words

Sometimes it is necessary to use magic words to be convincing. These magic words are meaningful and positive words. Advertisers know these positive and meaningful words intimately. It is very important for them to be able to use them. The words "New," "Renewed," "All Natural," "Most Effective" are the most appropriate examples of these magic words. Using these words, advertisers try to promote their products and thus make the advertisements more convincing for the liking of the products.

4. Use of Foot Technique

This technique is frequently used in the context of persuasion techniques. Processing way is quite simple. You make a person do something very small first because you think you can't refuse it. Once the other person has done so, you will try to get him to do more, provided that he is consistent within himself. First, you sell a product to a person at a very low price. Then you get him to buy a product at higher prices. In the first step, you attract him to yourself, so you convince him to buy it. In the second step, you convince yourself to buy products at a higher price. Their acceptance of a small thing will help you to fulfill the next big demand from you. After refusing the small request from the other party, you feel a duty to make a big request from the same person. This is usually the case in human relations. For example, you agree when your neighbor comes and asks you if you can keep an eye on the shop for a few hours. If your neighbor comes to ask you to look at the shop all day, you will feel responsible and probably accept it. This means that the technique of putting a foot on the door is successfully applied.

5. Use of Orientation from Big to Small

The tendency to ask from big to small is the exact opposite of the technique of putting a foot on the door. The salesperson makes an unrealistic request from the other person. Naturally, this demand doesn't correspond. However, the salesperson makes a request that is smaller than the same person. People feel responsible for such approaches, and they accept the offer. Since the request is small, by accepting it, people have the idea that they will help the salespeople and the technique of moving from big to small requests works.

6. Use of Reciprocity

Reciprocity is a term for mutual progress of a business. When a person does you a kindness, you feel the need to do him a favor. This is one example of reciprocity. For example, if someone bought you a gift on your birthday, you would try to pay back that gesture. This is more of a psychological approach because people don't forget the person who does something for them and tries to respond. For marketers, the situation is slightly different from human relations. Reciprocity takes place here in the form of a marketer offering you an interim extra discount" or "extra promotion... You are very close to buying the product introduced by the marketer you think offers a special offer.

7. Making Limits for Interviews

Setting a limit for negotiations is to provide an approach that will affect future copyrights. This is particularly effective when negotiating prices. For example, if you are trying to negotiate a price to sell a service, it might make more sense to start by opening the price from a higher number. Opening from a low number is not the right method because you have weakened your stretching share.

Even if the limitation for negotiations is not always useful, it's particularly useful in terms of price negotiation. Say the first number and get on with the bargaining advantage.

8. Limitation Technique

Restriction technique is one of the most powerful methods to influence human psychology. You can see this mostly in places selling products. For example, if a store has a discount on a particular product, it may limit it to 500 products. This limitation can be a true limitation or a part of the limitation technique. So you think that you will not find the product at that price again and you agree to buy that product at the specified price. The restriction technique is particularly useful in new products. As soon as a new product goes on sale, you can convince people to buy it for a limited time or by selling a limited quantity of products with extra promotions or discounts. People who think that the product will not be sold again at a similar price may choose to buy the product you have chosen thanks to the success of your persuasion technique. Persuasion techniques are not limited to these. Different techniques can provide more successful results in various fields. However, most of the techniques that we may encounter in our daily lives consist of the methods here. If you want to be a marketer, if you are trying to sell a product or service, you need to have detailed information about these techniques if you want to make them available.

Difference between Persuasion and Manipulation

There are many similarities between Persuasion and Manipulation as the two words confuse non-English individuals: Natives too. There are many comparisons between the two concepts, and because of the overlap, people think these two can be used interchangeably. There are convincing good people, and there are good manipulators. Both try to make sense and encourage others to accept their views. However, although there are similarities in manipulation to making a cousin or persuasive sibling, there are differences to be emphasized.

Persuasion

Persuasion is a behavior from someone else directed in a specific direction. You've managed to convince when you try to explain a certain way of behavior logically and correctly, and others accept your opinion that they think is of mutual benefit. If you have good marks on your test and you asked your mother for an expensive gift, you are trying to convince her to buy you a gift. This persuasion is convincing because it sees the logic behind your request and buys gifts. The salesperson is persuaded to sell a product or service to customers as he tries to create the need for the product or service in the customer's mind.

Manipulation

Manipulation is the act of exploiting the instability of others and misleading them to accept your point of view. Manipulation is not mutually beneficial, only advantageous for the manipulator. At the subconscious level, people strive to control each other in an organization or a family. Instead of persuading them for their benefit, they try to manipulate them. Manipulation can also be for the good of the person, even as a child's mother says that instead of eating all of them from the cookie jar, they can get a cookie. This creates the possibility of illusion, and your child can easily accept for fear of losing the jar without a single cookie. You manipulated the child's behavior for his good. Manipulation can also be bad, and manipulation is bad because the manipulator aims to trick and benefit from it.

The distinction between persuasion and manipulation

• Manipulation, managing others to benefit flawlessly.

• Persuading a particular person to change his or her thinking logically and rationally by reasoning with himself or by presenting arguments

• Manipulators can achieve short-term success, but people know who is manipulated and who convinces them in the long run.

• Persuasion is the art of achieving what you want by creating changes in the behavior of others, but it is manipulation. However, the difference is your intention.

• A person with good communication skills but malicious intent is dangerous because he can be a good manipulator.

Chapter 6 Manipulation Techniques

Manipulators are all around us. They could be your friends, neighbors, boss, colleagues, or even your life partner also. But it is not easy to identify them. Of course, they live with disappearing characters and personality traits........

No one moves with having a tag of psychopath or narcissist on their forehead.......but they can turn our lives into living hell.

They can use anyone as their prey to feed their anxious nature. These are disguised psychological vampires, and the only motive they have is to find a victim to satisfy their psychologically ill mentality.

We are not bound to become the next victim of their charm, but we can identify them with several traits and by knowing the techniques they use to manipulate. For manipulators, it is rewarding to learn the art of manipulation, and in reality, even we can also get the advantage of manipulating techniques to control the mind of others but still, it is important to draw an ethical line for testing your abilities.

It is a different debate here I am sharing you some very common techniques to manipulate people.

Mirroring Technique:

This very famous manipulating technique involves two steps:

Initially, you need to act as a mirror image of the person whom you are going to manipulate, and in the second step, the process gets reversed. Behavior coping is a basic tool for this technique. Copy every quality you notice in your subject from body language to tonality, and from face and hand gestures to communicating and behaving abilities.....just do everything in their way, and they will notice you and they will start to feel more close and connected with you. And this will be the right time to implement further manipulation methods on the vulnerable subject.

Manipulation requires the complete trust of your subject; otherwise, it becomes really hard to manipulate anyone. Mirroring is a slow but highly effective technique to make you closer to your subject, and other techniques will easily influence the mind of the subject but don't consider it a kind of magic to be done within seconds or minutes it may get prolonged to hours and days.

CAUTION: perform mirroring with as carefully as possible otherwise, your mirroring attempts could make the subject suspicious about you. And once you lose the connection, it is near impossible to recover the early position.

Love Bombing Technique:

But love bombing is not as simple as this proverb; it is a complex and typical technique usually used by Narcissists.

Manipulators use it in the early phases of interaction to show positive affection, interest, and harmony with the subject. Being extremely nice to the victim generates an overwhelmingly positive attitude inside the subject for you. Originally you set an emotional trap for the subject and grip the sentiments of the subject easy to manipulate.

This technique is not for everyone, but it is highly applicable for the people who have a lack of love and happiness in their lives. And they always remain in need of getting the attention and care from anywhere.

CAUTION: it is important to keep your intentions and objectives hidden and don't start to manipulate your subject just after quick love bombing but give them some time to become used to.

Good Listener Technique:

Please understand the tricks of manipulation. It is not just about hacking someone's brain and makes them do whatever you wish. It is about grabbing the trust and better understanding of your subject. And to understand anyone, it is essential to know them. The best way to know a person is listening to them.

Becoming a good listener for your subject establishes an illusion of comfort and friendship between both of you. The subject starts trusting you and feels relaxed to discuss their daily routine, personal and professional issues, and their social and love life with you. Their life becomes an open book for you. The only things you need to do are listening to them quietly or just pretend as a good listener in front of them.

You not only need to listen and forget everything, but for manipulating it is also required to make them realize that you care for them by repeating their discussed information in a wisely manner.

CAUTION: Good listening technique is not all about listening and then replicating everything like a parrot but use the important part of information according to the requirements of the situation.

Trapping Personality Technique:

Life is a bed of roses for beautiful people. But it is a half-truth, beauty attracts the eyes, but the heart responds to the personality. Admiring beauty and personality is something in human nature. And using the charisma and charm of your personality wisely is the skill requirements for manipulation.

Beauty counts, but still, you need to work on your personality. Positive attitude with perfect body language, approachable and welcoming gesture and command on word power are the weapons to hunt the subject for manipulation. Always be a self-confident person and make people feel great being with you. It will help you to win every race of life individually, personally, and professionally.

CAUTION: Avoid over doings and never become overconfidence because no one likes a brash person regardless of how attractive, charming, and well personality he has.

Fear And Relief Technique:

It is documented and highly researched technique for manipulation. Even this technique causes so much anxiety and stress, but anyhow it is extremely adequate. Fear and relief technique manipulate people by playing with their emotions.

It is a simple two steps method:

1.   Firstly set a fear for something in your subjects mind to make him feel up guarded and unprotected.

2.   In the second part give your subject an offer to provide relief against their fear.

But what actually can make a person scared is the most challenging part of this technique. Seriously it is not possible to make people feared from some kind of evil dead and zombie kind of things. You better search keenly for their real fears and the situations and sentiments that can make them scared. Analyzing the subject properly reveals their terrors and frightening to you. Just be little creative and use their relationships, career, aims, and goals of life for frightening them.

CAUTION: It is not only about making your subject feared, but you must have the solution to rescue them from their consternation.

82

Guilty Approach Technique:

Nobody wants to become a villain or desires to become guilty. So try to understand the power of making people feel guilty and use this technique for your best. You create a psychological effect to obligate make people feel guilty of their some kind of act or behavior by using some emotionally catchy and pinching sentences like "I was never expecting this kind of evil/cruel gesture from you", or "I always helped you in every situation no matter what it was, but you disappointed me."

No one wants to spoil their good image, and ultimately the subject feels like fulfilling your demand. And at this point, you can plant your theory in their subconscious and let them move with the flow.

CAUTION: you have to be very careful with this technique; otherwise, you might be suspected of being manipulating people.

All these manipulating techniques work to provide you easy prey. It is not possible to get the same results every time with a technique. Every time you manipulate a different person with almost different qualities and flaws. Sometimes it just happens within no time, and sometimes it takes a long and exhausting period of implementing the tricks on the victim.

In addition to all these techniques, you have to combine your looks and verbal communication skills also. Crucially you need to work on:

Technique + Verbal communication + Appearance = Perfect manipulating personality

Application Of Manipulation Techniques

Everyone considers manipulation as a real danger. We feel scared of manipulators and try to identify them for our protection. But still, all of us become the victims of manipulation almost every day.

Yes, we are surrounded with people, groups, and industries who are manipulating us 24 x 7 for their hidden interests. The surprising thing about this kind of manipulation is "no complains about being manipulated or being fool".

Manipulation is converted into art now. In this era of technology and science, it is becoming essential to manipulate people for certain reasons. These reasons are sometimes good, but most of the times not. Applications of manipulation in the field of psychology and medical are acceptable because occasionally, it is essential to manipulate a mentally ill patient for their recovery and treatments.

Here are some other applications of manipulation we observe in our daily life and never complained about these:

Marketing And Manipulation:

Have you ever experienced yourself singing, dancing, and performing some kind of unreal stunts while opening a can of a soft drink?????

Or after eating a bar of chocolate, you ever transferred to an amazing world where everything is made up of chocolate???

Ok, let's change the question....

Have you ever seen girls attacking you just after spraying a deodorant or body spray???

In reality, nothing happens like that......Agree!!!!!

All these are manipulating tact's to convince and attract you towards that particular product. Marketing is a technique to boost business and converting viewers into customers to increase sale. All these marketing tricks not only sell a product directly but in actual they manipulate your mind with an experience that appeals us, and we move our hands toward our wallets to bring out money for observing the same kind of sensation and transformation.

But sadly things never play out as they do in commercials and movies. Marketers not only manipulate customers in only a fictional way as I mentioned before, but they consider marketing as love or war where all is fair. They use manipulation, or you may call it brainwashing also to sell their products by using some marketing manipulation techniques as advertisements and marketing tools.

- **product placement:** Marketers insert their product in TV dramas, shows, and movies for promotion, and it works. It is a powerful strategy to relate a product with your favorite program or personality.

- **promotions:** Bargaining is something that fascinates us. Marketers manipulate the price of products and present a scam offer. They raise the prices of products before a sale and then implement eye-catching and tempting discount signs like 50% off, Sale, Buy one get one free, etc.

- **emotions:** We are emotional beings, and marketers get benefits by manipulating our emotions. They create an emotional and sentimental story that we love to see again and again and try to relate with it by building positive feelings with the brands. Although marketers also manipulate with generating negative feelings, fear and anxiety-like; promotions are ending soon, limited stock, and one time offer, etc.

- **expert opinions:** All of us observe some kind of expert-based promotions of certain products. In these advertisements, they present doctors or professionals promoting products with some serious names that give a feel of an institute. Do any of us ever think about their credibility? But unconsciously start following their advice considering that product as reliable and recommended by the experts.

- **social proofs:** sometimes, marketers use the same strategy of expert opinion by involving common people. Mostly this promotion tact is the main part of online shopping and promotions. Online reviews are 80% effective for the next purchase, and we trust these reviews for our next purchase.

Media And Manipulation:

There was a time media persons remain in search of news for most of the time, but now the situation is changed. Now the media produces the news. They provide us nothing but distortion and fabrication. It is nice to think media as a trustworthy and reliable medium, but this is not true. They have the power to change a useless and foolish kind of information into highly trending and breaking news by using catchy titles and attractive headlines. In the mean, while they convert an important hot issue into a completely vulnerable subject.

In a nut, shell media is shaping up everything we hear, watch or read. Media has changed its medium from being informative to being more entertaining. The better the entertainment, the more profit media channels will generate.

In actual, media is manipulation with our subconscious. We think that we are keeping in touch with the happening all around the world, but originally we just click and click for the profit generation and benefits of folks. Some techniques media use to manipulate us are:

• **know the public very well:** complete information about the subject is the first step of manipulation. Media has all the information about every single person thanks to our modern autocracy. In simple words, unfortunately, the system knows us and provides a strong base to media agencies for manipulation.

- **emotional appeal:** Media controls the thoughts of viewers and keeps them far away from critical thinking. Media appeals to our emotions and triggers sentiments of the public.

- **gradualism:** Media creates awareness slowly and starts preparing the public for "big news". This, in actual, helps media to manipulate the public for accepting a socially unjust situation. This gradualism slowly but effectively dilutes the resistance and agitation from the public for a particular issue.

- **adults or children:** Media treats their viewers like children. They consider the audience so much immature to handle the reality that is why they use sugarcoated modulations, actions, and characters to generate a compliant and submissive reaction.

- **distraction:** Media manipulates the minds of people by flooding the news about trivial issues and occupies their minds completely. The reason behind this strategy is to deviate public attention from real issues and stopping them from questioning certain issues.

Politics And Manipulation:

Do you know why you cast a vote for a party or politician?

Do you know about their real policies and planning for the betterment of the country?

Or it was just about observing their campaigns, TV interviews, and live sessions?

Politics is broken. Yes, it is a dirty game where people/politicians manipulate the sentiments, emotions, and views of the public for the success of their party and to rule the country. They create nasty political ads to generate polarization for the ideology to cling with their opinions and agendas.

The most powerful techniques these politicians use to manipulate public opinion are:

• **external threats:** By creating outside enemy, they generate fear in public and manipulate them to go with their foreign policies because they can deal so much effectively with outer threats.

• **excessive use of ''protect'':** The word ''protect'' generates a kind of safe and sound situation regarding anything. Politicians use it excessively to make us feel that they care for us. They manipulate us by saying, again and again, the same sentence as; we need to protect X. here X is anything from women's rights, minority rights, religion, moral values, to social, educational, and welfare rights.

• **disgrace the opponent:** Politics is a real nasty. By disgracing the opponent in politics, these political manipulators achieve many hidden benefits. People stop caring about the policies, manifesto, and agendas of opponents. And the feel of compassion for the rival just gets disappeared. Politicians spread negative rumors and information related to their opponents, blur the opponent's personal life and question their integrity and patriotism to manipulate the public for personal benefits.

Chapter 7 How to Manipulate People

There are going to be certain times in your life when you will find that manipulation is going to come in handy. While you know that it is so important to practice in as many scenarios as you can, there are going to be ones that you will find manipulation will be the most useful. In this chapter, we are going to focus on the best places where you can use the skills of manipulation so that you can get ahead and really benefit from the things that you have learned so far.

Business Negotiations

When it comes to working on some negotiations in business, it is easy to see how you want to make sure that you can get your way. Getting your own way will usually mean that you want to close a better deal, one that is going to be highly favorable to your own company. Closing these deals, and making sure that they are in your favor, will mean that your company is able to get most, if not all, of the things that it is asking for, and that you will barely have to deal with any inconveniences in the process to do this.

There are a lot of things that you can negotiate during these meetings, such as better terms on the deals, better pricing on the services, and more, and if you use your skills in manipulation, you are more likely to get the whole thing to work in your favor.

When it comes to negotiating on some better deals for the business, you will find that manipulation is a very powerful tool for you to use. Whether others like to admit to this or not, negotiations are rarely fair, and there is usually going to be a person who comes out on top. You want to make sure that the person who comes out on top is you.

When you use manipulation in these efforts, it means that you are easily able to dominate the conversation, without the other person even realizing it. When this happens, others in the negotiation are more likely to give in without even doing a fight, because they think they are getting something good out of it as well. Because of this, and all of the good benefits that you can get from this, you should bring out the manipulation skills that you learn as much as possible when you are working with a business negotiation.

Closing Sales

If you are at all involved in a sales process at some point, then you know that it is not always easy to close sales. If you work in retail, for example, you likely notice that many of the people who come into your store are dreaming and looking around, and sometimes, they won't be prepared to buy anything. Because of this, it can sometimes be valuable to know how to manipulate people as you can encourage them to spend money that they did not otherwise intend to spend.

What this means is that when you get the other person to purchase something through your manipulation techniques, it results in more sales for the business. If you are the one who owns the company, you know how important this is. If you are an employee, you know that effective numbers of sales, and good sales strategies, means that you are more likely to be respected by your employer, and then you can make it up the ladder of the company.

If you are in a sales position that is considered business to business, then you know that manipulation is so important. People who end up going to a meeting with you are likely interested in what you are going to offer, but they could also be shopping around to a few different companies at the same time, and you need to find ways that will put your business ahead of all the other choices that they are considering.

Knowing how to use the right skills of manipulation at any level of sales means that they can close more deals and that they will be left with happier customers. This only means that good things are going to be available for you in the future.

Getting Prices That Are Better

You can use manipulation from the other side of the perspective as well. If you are the customer and knowing how to manipulate during this time can be highly valuable. As you know, many times the salespeople have been given some room to negotiate with their customers in order to encourage sales. This means that if you are willing to use some manipulation and work with them, you can get a special and better deal. You are able just to take the price, but wouldn't it be much better for you to go through and get a better price if you are able to.

Being effective at manipulation means that you can easily manipulate companies to give you the best in deals for services and products. By promising them your praise and services, for example, you can essentially get them in the palm of your hand. They become far more willing to communicate with their managers and negotiate the best possible deal for you so that you will actively buy from them. Salespeople, especially those who are based on commission, are always eager to close a deal. This allows you to use manipulation in order to get the deal to close in your favor.

Leading the Desired Lifestyle That You Want

Each person has a goal about the desired lifestyle that they would like to have—but the lifestyle that you have right now, and the one that you desire, might not always be the same thing. However, the good thing about using manipulation is that you are able to use it to help you get to the desired lifestyle. There are a lot of ways that you can do this—you just need to learn how to make it work.

Let's say that right now you are living in a house that you are renting, and you want to buy your own home at some point—but right now, the types of homes that you are the most interested in purchasing are not within the price that you can purchase. However, with the right kind of manipulation, you may find that you are able to get a better deal, putting you into the home of your dreams sooner as you would like. This can work with any of the big-ticket items that you would like to purchase, such as cars.

Another way that this can work is with some of the relationships that you are in. If you are someone who would like to find a new group of friends, the friends who are going to help you reflect your new lifestyle, you may find that working with manipulation is going to help you out. You can also use the art of persuasion to convince others to become your friends and spend time with you—and from that, you will then have the friends that you need to live this new lifestyle.

Take this a step further and see how it can work with some of your intimate relationships. If this kind of relationship doesn't look like the one that you would like, then you can bring in some manipulation and see if it is possible to make the right changes towards a better relationship. If you want to have more romance, for example, you would spend some time with fancier places or people.

Getting Out of Things

Have you ever gotten into a situation where you were asked to do something, but you didn't have any want to do it? All of the time we are going to be signed up for things, or given offers, that we aren't really that interested in—and sometimes, it can feel difficult to turn these things down in a polite manner. Depending on who is asking for the favor, you may feel obligated to help them out with it.

However, once you learn how to work with manipulation a bit more, you will find that this is not as big of a problem for you anymore. You may even find that this is a good place to start when it comes to practicing your manipulation. You can bring it up any time that you get stuck doing something that you would rather not be doing.

Not only are you able to use manipulation for your benefit to get out of the reunions or things that family and friends want you to help out with, but you can also use it at work as well. If your boss went and signed you up for something that you don't want to do, you can use manipulation to convince them to let you get out of it, or you can convince someone else to go and do the work for you.

You can use manipulation in any manner that you would like to make sure that you are able to live the life that you want. It can help you to get the business negotiations to work the way that you want, to help you get the friendships, relationships, and to get yourself out of the things that you don't want to do. There are just so many different things that you are able to use manipulation with, and this can be a great way to ensure that you have the life that you have always dreamed about.

Chapter 8 Deception

There are ways people use deception; sometimes, the deception is self-deception, while at other times, other people deceive someone else for selfish gains like money or getting confidential information that should not be shared.

Self-deception does not only involve lying to ourselves but also consists of the mind playing tricks on us. With lying, someone is aware of the truth but chooses not to use the truth but instead lie while self-deception people convince themselves unconsciously that a lie is a truth. In self-deception, a person does not realize when they are telling a lie. There are various types of self-deception which include:

1.   Functional self-deception – a person will lie to themselves and even go ahead to convince himself that what he just did is not wrong. A person in this will try to turn a lie into a truth so that it can suit them best. A person who continues to continually deceive themselves this way does not face any risks because they will not see the need for taking a chance no matter how beneficial the risk is. They will convince themselves that the risk is not worth taking.

2.   Value and believe - a person here deceives themselves that the more expensive something is, the more valuable it is. They place worthiness at the value level. If something does not seem valuable to them, they will not go for it. This might make such a person continue chasing things that are valuable but not helpful to them. They think the difficult it is to attain it the worthy it is, so much

time may be lost while trying to get something that wasn't going to help them in any way.

3.   Consolatory self-deception - in this, somebody refuses to be accountable for anything and instead continually tries to find the nearest person to blame for everything. For such people, nothing is ever their fault; it's always the other person's fault that something didn't work in a certain way. Such a person is unlikely ever to face their problems because they do not acknowledge them, to begin with.

4.   Lying to others to assure yourself is also another form of self-deception. You tend to make small lies when talking to people until the lies become your truth somehow. Such people lie to others until they also end up forgetting what the truth was, to begin with. The lie becomes so real that even the truth now becomes a lie. The mind somehow captures the dishonesty, and therefore, the truth is easily forgotten.

The other deception, which is very dangerous involves offenders trying to deceive people in a criminal way. The scammers will get their targeted victims, who will cheat and up sometimes robbing them of a lot of money, getting very confidential information, and sometimes even risking the victim's life. Such offenders are criminals who are continually sought after by the law enforcers. Sometimes they are able to get away with it but at the expense of living the victim in a tragedy of loss and having to deal with the recovery of whatever they have lost from the perpetrators.

Art of deception has been well mastered by some individuals to exploit people into disclosing confidential and personal information, which may be used for scheming purposes. The art of deception is a way of brainwash people to achieve a sure selfish thing. It involves social engineering manipulation, which is the psychological tricking of other people for them to do or disclose their personal information. A lot of malicious activities happen when people interact. People are tricked into making security errors and giving out the very sensitive information that may work against them in the long run.

Social engineering attacks happen when people take a lot of sensitive issues for granted. An offender will first carry out his investigation on his targeted victim and gather as much information as he could get. The information may include social security details that the victim doesn't think is very important. The offender will then try to befriend the victim and gain his trust before proceeding to expose the information by either releasing it or sharing with other sources that may have hired him.

The Attacks May Involve the Following Life Cycle

• Preparation – an offender gets their intended victim, gets all the information needed to base the attack, finds the best strategy or method to carry out the attack.

• Approach – making friends with the intended victim, faking a believable story so that the victim may be free with them,

• Gathering more information – this involves tricking the already made friend who is the victim to give more additional information, delivery of the attack after all the information has been collected, and there is no loophole, destruction of data.

- Sealing the deal - the offender erases any evidence that may tie him to the crime, covers all the track to ensure that his attack is not easily traceable, Making a natural exit as if nothing happened and as if he is not aware of anything related to those activities.

- The most dangerous aspect of this whole social engineering thing is that it is dependent on human mistakes or recklessness. The software and operating system are highly efficient, but when somebody makes a mistake, there is nothing that can prevent this attack from happening. It is very difficult to predict human errors and, therefore, the vulnerabilities.

- Social engineering can happen at any time, anywhere in the world, as long as there is human interaction. Below is a list of some of the most and widely known social engineering attacks that exist.

Social Engineering Techniques

• Baiting is a deliberate attempt to try and provoke someone or something. Baiting attacks involve giving fake promises to provoke the greed or curiosity of the victim. A victim is lured into a trap where their information is stolen, or their system is inflicted with malware. The most common type of baiting involves the use of media to distribute malware. An example of this is when an offender intentionally put a malware-infected flash where the victim is most likely to access like in a mall, in the washrooms, or parks where the victim can quickly get hold of it. The bait has an original look and has a label that may indicate things that the victim is most likely to be interested in. When the victim picks up the flash, and due to curiosity inserts the flash inside a home or work computer, there will be an automatic installation of the malware on the system.

• Scareware involves constant scaring of people with false alarms or fabricated threats. The victim is made to think that his system has a malware infection, which may make them install software that is not really needed for the victim but may be useful to the offender or even be deceived into installing the malware itself without them realizing that it is malware. Scareware is also called deception software or "Fraudware." The most famous or used shareware includes the pop-up banners that pop up on someone's browser when they are on the screen that screams that the computer is infected and may need to be cleaned. What the pop-up banner offers a person is the installation of a tool that may be malware of may be infected with malware. You may also be directed to a site that has infections, and when you get to the site, the computer now becomes infected. Often scareware is distributed as a pop-up banner in the mails as a spam mail or even as a buy offer to buy things online with very low prices or even in the form of very catchy promotions. If someone does all or one of the above, their computer will be infected.

• Pretexting – the deception here is wisely crafted with trickery lies involved. An offender will trick the victim by engaging them and asking for sensitive, confidential information so that the offender can be able to perform a specific task for the victim. Usually, the task includes something that may help the victim. To be able to achieve this, the attacker will first try to engage the victim by impersonation. They may pretend to be a family member, friend, co-worker, police, bank official, or any person with authority to make such inquisitions. The offender will begin by asking questions that are intended to gather a victim's real identity from which they will then be able to gather confidential information. The pretext may ask questions about the social number details pretending to be the police, and later use the features to access all the data belonging to the victim. This scam is used to gather the most detailed information that is supposed to be a top-secret, and that could quickly bring a person down. The information may include social number details, bank statements, personal address, personal number, phone's recording, and even information that gives a person their security. With this information lying on the wrong hands, destruction is very easy, and that's why it is essential to be sure of who you are sharing your details with.

• Phishing is one of the most well-known social engineering attack types. Phishing involves mail, text messages that are intended to create a sense of fear, curiosity, and urgency to the victims. When the victims are at this phase of fear and curiosity, the offender makes the victim reveal their most sensitive information by clicking on links of the most dangerous websites or even by accessing malware-infected websites. The example of this scam is an online service provider tricks the user into thinking that they have violated the policy and need an essential password change with immediate effect. To change the password, one is required to follow a specific link that usually leads them to a dangerous website that looks exactly as the real website or the actual legit version of the site, and then the victim will be trusting enough to enter the relevant information plus password. Once this information is fed on the website its sent and immediately gets to the offender, since most of these scam emails are usually the same or most likely to be the same, and only changed in several areas to make them seem more authentic and yet sent to everyone, it's very easy for them to be detected and blocked before they get to a lot of innocent victims. The mail servers should try tracing them so that they are blocked on time because they have access to threat sharing forums.

• Spear phishing is a version of the phishing scam, and attackers in this scam choose specific individuals or companies. They fake the messages based on a person's well-known identity or character, positions they hold at their workplace, and people that the victim well knows so that it is easily believable. Spearfishing requires so much time and work for the attacker and takes longer for the attacker to implement. This is because it is harder for them to gather everything and also apply, although it's also the best rewarding method for the attacker. A spear-phishing attack may involve someone pretends to be the company's IT guy, and he may send emails to a specific or several employees. The mail is written precisely as an IT guy would and also have the same signature as the IT guy. It is, therefore, very easy for the mail recipients to think it's an authentic message because of how detailed and genuine it looks. The email may persuade the recipients to change their password by following a link that the offender intends them to follow for them to be able to capture the company's details. There are several ways that people can avoid and stop this kind of scams.

- Vishing – sometimes, the attackers are not always using the internet to scam, but then other scammers will use the phone calls. What the scammers will do is create an interactive voice response system of a certain company. They will then manipulate people to call using the toll-free number. When people fall into this trick, they will enter their details before making the calls, and therefore, the attackers will get access to their information in this way.

- Tailgating – Here, attackers will get help from someone on the inside who can access the information on their behalf or even who can tip them on various issues.

- Quid pro quo – this involves people impersonating the technical support team. They will make calls to a particular company and pretend to be trying to solve a technical issue. The offender will try to solve un existing hitches through the phone call by making the victim do precisely as they want or intend them to. This kind of scam involves a reward from the offender in exchange for the information they will get.

Social Engineering Prevention

Social engineering is a scam intended to manipulate people by playing with their emotions by creating fear or curiosity for the attackers to be able to gather information. There are, therefore, cautions that a person can take in order to avoid these scams. Emails received should be taken with great caution, reading, analyzing, and getting to know every detail before acting on them. Be alert of all the pop-ups, promotions or adverts, and any digital information that is just at the disposal.

Improving emotional intelligence is the most significant prevention of any manipulation. The attackers will try to play with your emotions; what they most want from you is to make you fearful, guilty, and anxious. A person with high emotional intelligence cannot be played in this manner and is therefore safe from manipulation.

Be cautious of your environment before accessing your account or any activity on the internet. One glance at your computer from the wrong person might significantly expose your confidential information.

Avoid and stop opening emails from sources that are not well known to you. If you are not familiar with the sender, you should not feel obligated to reply to an mail. And even though you know the sender but the message seems suspicious, or you do not understand the message, it's good to do a follow up before acting on the mail. To do this confirmation, you may call them through their phones to hear directly from them, or instead of following the link; you should go directly to the server's original site to be sure. It's good to always remember that emails are hacked all the time, and even though the source of the email may be genuine, he may have been hacked himself, and the attackers used his mail to scam you.

Multifactor method – the essential information for an attacker is user credentials. The multifactor authentication enables a person to secure their account so that in case the system is compromised; your mind is still safe. The security information of the report should always be safeguarded.

Being careful of all those too good to be genuine offers is very important. Attackers know how to play with your mind, and suggestions are very enticing. Next time before you click an offer link, it's good to pause and think because you might be protecting yourself from a massive scam. You may decide to look the offer up on google to find out if the offer is indeed genuine or not.

Keeping your computer's antivirus updated is also very important. Regularly updating the antivirus should be a norm or downloading a new antivirus on a daily basis. Then the next thing should be continually checking the computers to make sure that the system has no infections.

Attackers are very daring because they will get a person's phone number and make the victim the most irresistible offer. They are very friendly because they intend to make you trust them. Sometimes they will ask the victims for money in order for the victim to get the offer, which is usually much valuable than the money they are asking for. This art of deception is called a Fraud. But then the extreme of deception is when attackers decide to use psychological games of deceit with the victim who is now the social engineering.

Sometimes attackers do not just manipulate for financial gains. Sometimes the attackers will manipulate to gather information. This manipulation sometimes involves even having your friends manipulating you for them to access your password.

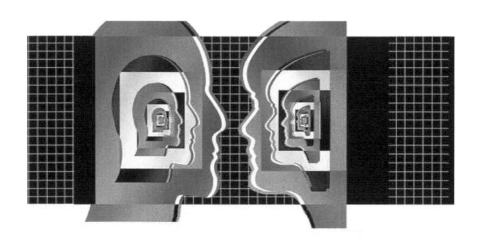

Chapter 9 Using NLP to Manage People

When it comes to managing people effectively, it's important that you first understand the non-verbal cues they provide, in order to be able to apply your skills toward influencing them. This is an important principle in applying the NLP technique. Following are a few NLP techniques that can allow you to influence people's perception and thinking:

Deciphering eye movements

The reason it is important to understand the meaning of eye movements is that each eye movement tells its own tale. For instance, when you're searching for the right word, or trying to remember a name, you automatically move your eyes in a certain way (most likely, squinting). Rolling the eyes signals contempt, or exasperation. Winking indicates flirtation, or a joke. Widening the eyes signals surprise, or shock; even extreme excitement. We've discussed earlier, how eye movements are also implicated in other facial expressions. In fact, the eyes can reveal much more about people's mental and emotional status, all on their own.

Once you understand what other people's thought processes are, you can accurately follow a course of action or dialogue which acknowledges the unspoken response, as signaled by the eyes. And as you may know, eye movements complement other forms of communication such as hand movements, speech and, as stated elsewhere in this book and above, facial expressions. Dilation of the pupils, breathing, angle of the body, position of the hands – all these are complementary to the spoken message. Still, eye movement is very important in communication, because every movement is influenced by particular senses, as well as different parts of the brain.

Here is how you can generally interpret eye movement:

Visual responsiveness

• Eyes upward, then towards the right:

Whenever a person tilts eyes upward and then to the right, it means that the person is formulating a mental picture.

• Eyes upward, then towards the left:

Whenever a person tilts eyes upward, followed by an eye movement to the left, it means the person is recalling a certain image.

• Eyes looking straight ahead:

Whenever someone focuses directly in front of them, as though looking at a point in the distance, this indicate that the person is not focused on anything in particular. That is the look often referred to as 'glazed'.

Auditory Responsiveness.

- Eyes looking towards the right:

When a person's eyes shift straight towards the right, it means the person is in the process of constructing a sound.

- Eyes looking towards the left:

When a person's eyes shift straight towards the left, it indicates that the person is recalling a sound.

Audio-digital responsiveness

- Eyes looking downward, then switching to the left:

When someone drops their eyes and then proceeds to turn their eyes to the left, this signals that the person is engaged in internal dialogue.

- Eyes looking right down then left to right:

When a person looks downward and then proceeds to turn their eyes to the left and then, to the right in consecutive movements, it means the person is engaged in negative self-talk.

Kinesthetic responsiveness:

Here, the person looks directly down, only to turn the eyes to the right. That is an indication that the person is evaluating emotional status. This further indicates

that the person is not at ease.

Verbal responses:

Rhythmic speech

The idea here is not to be poetic as you speak, but to speak at a regular pace. The recommended pace of speaking is equated to the heartbeat, say, between 45 and 72 beats per minute. At that pace, you are likely to sustain the listener's attention and establish greater receptivity to what you're saying. While normal conversational speed averages about 140 words per minute, slowing down a little and taking time to pause is highly effective as a means of sustaining people's attention. Your regular cadence should be punctuated by fluctuations in tone and emphasis, in order not to sound monotonous.

Repeating key words

When you are trying to influence someone, there are key words or phrases which that carry additional weight as far as your message is concerned. This method of speaking is a way of embedding the message in the listener and subtly suggesting that your message is valid and worthy of reception. Repeating key words also suggests commitment, conviction and mastery of the subject matter.

Using strongly suggestive language

Use language that is positive and supportive of what you are saying, using a selection set of strong, descriptive words or phrases. As you do this, you should observe the person you are speaking to closely, in a way that makes them feel as though you are seeing right through them and aware of what they are thinking. Don't be invasive about this, or aggressive. Merely suggest, by way of your gaze that you have a keen appreciation of what makes people tick. This places you in a dominant position, especially when accompanied by dominant body language, like "steepling" (see section on hand gestures). It helps to use suitable, complementary body language as you speak, to subtly underscore the message.

Touching the person lightly, as you speak

Touching the person as you speak to them draws their attention to you in a relaxed and familiar way. By employing this technique, you're preparing the listener to absorb what you are saying to them; a way of programming attentiveness. Those engaging in inter-gender conversations in the workplace should take great care with this technique, as it can lead to misunderstandings.

Using a mixture of "hot" and "vague" words

"Hot" words are those that tend to provoke specific sensations in the listener. When you are using them to influence someone's thinking, it is advisable to use them in a suitable pattern. Examples of phrases containing hot words are: it means; feel free; see this; because; hear this. The effect of employing these words and phrases is that you're directing influencing the listener's state of mind, including how that person feels, imagines and perceives. You're also appealing to the sense most prevalent in the listener's perceptive style (as observed through the movement of their eyes). For example, the phrase "hear this" will appeal to those who indicate a tendency to respond most actively to auditory stimuli.

Using the interspersal technique

The interspersal technique is the practice of stating one thing, while hoping to impress on the listener something entirely different.

The techniques just described form strategies in the service of influencing people. They're not intended to force a viewpoint, or to control people's behavior for nefarious ends. These techniques are intended to modify undesirable behaviors which may be resulting in workplace difficulties, including the failure of staff to work well together, or to complete team projects. They're also extremely helpful in the context of relationships with young people and children, whether at home, or in a learning environment. Techniques of subtle manipulative effect like those described, though capable of influencing people and their behavior, don't amount to anything even approaching coercion. The person being spoken to chooses all responses and is merely influenced, or steered toward those responses.

Chapter 10 Dark Psychology

Now that you have a suitable baseline for understanding dark psychology's nature and practice, remembering that practice is at the core of dark psychology's nature, that it exists to be **used** more than studied, you are ready to start learning about the tools employed by dark psychology practitioners the world over. You will additionally remember that, while the terms "tools," "techniques," and "methods" will be used interchangeably throughout, it is best to think of these sub-crafts of dark psychology as first and foremost **tools**, because tools, again, are objects meant to be **used**.

Manipulation

In many ways, beyond containing within its deception, manipulation hints at and implies the existence of the other tools of dark psychology. In many ways, dark psychology is ultimately a **method** for better manipulation.

If you google "dark psychology" and click through the first few articles, you will see immediately that almost every source on dark psychology uses manipulation several to many times, and that in most cases it is a subheading within the article, or even in the subtitle to the article itself! This illustrates how significant manipulation is too dark psychology and how broadly the two are connected. In fact, as was hinted at above, manipulation could itself be split into several subcategories. Obviously, one would be **deception**, which was already covered. Otherwise, their **machiavellianism, reverse psychology, semantics,** all of which could be described to some extent or another as kinds of **covert-aggression.**

All forms of manipulation could be described as covert-aggression because manipulation is inherently an aggressive social tactic. If a driver shouts aggressively at another car to "MOVE!" or because that driver of that other car cut him or her off, that driver is aggressive because he or she wants his or her will to take precedence over the other driver's will. He or she shouts "MOVE!" because he or she wants the other driver to move, in other words, and manipulation functions the same way. Unlike other forms of aggression, though, it has a secondary aim: avoid the detection.

This also speaks to the dark or sinister core of manipulation; it is always about power, and power is always, on some levels, angry and forceful. This is as true for semantic manipulation, a technique that can seem not just easy-going but even agreeable, as it is for Machiavellianism, a worldview named for a famously cynical and power-hungry author and politician.

To slow it down so as not to miss anything, we will unpack the concept of semantic manipulation. Chances are, you have experienced this method of manipulation in your life several times. It is, stated simply when a person insists that he or she understands words to mean something other than what they normally mean as a means of re-framing and controlling social interactions. Say, for example, a couple has a conversation where one, a man, tells his partner, a woman, that he really doesn't think very highly of her mother. Perhaps this was already an attempt at dark persuasion, which is coming up next, but perhaps not. Either way, the woman, understandably, gets upset with him for saying such a cruel thing out of nowhere. His response to her anger, however, disarms her immediately. He, calmly, tells her he didn't mean it negatively. "Thinking highly," he explains, means to him thinking that a person is imposing and scary. By "not thinking highly" of her mother, he meant that he saw her as a friendly and welcoming person with whom he could speak openly. In response, if he is successful, his partner becomes immediately less angry, believing herself to have misinterpreted his words. You can see how this can be useful on a basic level but also consider how, applied repeatedly, it creates a pattern wherein the practitioner is free from all criticism and looked at as a flawless, golden kind of person.

As you can see, deception is all-over the above methods. It is fundamental to most practices of manipulation. However it is important to note, that deception is **not** synonymous with telling lies. In fact, telling lies is just one subcategory of deception, which contains all manners of withholding, skewing or twisting of the truth **along with** the outright telling of falsehoods. This distinction is important because in many instances telling lies is nor the most efficient neither the most useful form of deception. Lies are often easier to detect and harder to pass-off than forms of deception that meld the truth with lies, or that function only as an absence of truth.

You probably have a passing understanding of reverse psychology, namely that it is telling a person to do one thing, so they do another. Well, it does run deeper than that, which seems to imply that people make decisions on a binary. This is not the case normally. One of the most brilliant things about reverse psychology is that, when deployed correctly, it is, itself, the impetus for limiting another's thought to a "yes or no" question. In order to make that friend come along, he or she says, as if a normal statement, "You probably don't want to go. You're not really into **fun** like that." In that scenario, the dark psychologist is using reverse psychology, clearly, but what he or she is also doing is turning the question of whether or not to go to the beach into a question of whether or not that friend is fun. So, of course, the friend decides to go to the beach!

Hopefully, you're starting to get a picture of the varieties and permutations of manipulation as they function on people in the world. From the above, you should also get the idea that, while there are distinct words for different kinds of manipulation, ultimately they blend together and can be used in tandem with one another. There is no reason why an attempt at semantic manipulation can't be employed along with reverse psychology, perhaps as a means of framing the yes/no dichotomy through which the target of the manipulation is meant to think. Likewise, it is impossible to imagine Machiavellianism without covert-aggression, and fairly difficult to imagine the reverse. That is all to say that manipulation is ultimately a fluid thing, as you will see with the rest of the tools laid out in this chapter and, admittedly, with most ideas you engage with every day. Although these things are "dark," they function like anything else. Taken in reality, in their actual **use**, these concepts all blend together.

Persuasion

A note before diving into the skillset known as persuasion – persuasion, in fact, exists in two varieties. There is, on the one hand, regular everyday persuasiveness. This is the persuasion people are talking about when they, for instance, reference persuasive writing techniques. It can also contain the social pressure of the ethically or morally-minded variety. On the other hand, though, and more in line with the topic of this book, is **dark persuasion**. It is the persuasiveness of con men, corrupt politicians, and amoral attorneys. All groups of people who are, you guessed it, routinely practitioners of dark psychology.

As was said above, manipulation can be viewed in a sense as a partial umbrella term for all of dark psychology. This **is** true, but in another sense, dark persuasion can itself be viewed as an umbrella term for all of dark psychology, which would mean that manipulation is itself contained in **it.** How, you ask, can manipulation and persuasion both contain each other? The answer, of course, is that categorizations are contingent and incomplete things a lot of the time. This ambiguity, however, is productive for the practitioner of dark psychology. Think back to the introduction, where the link between the power of the world and dark psychology was laid out. You will recall that knowledge of dark psychology has remained for elite eyes only – that is to say, obscured to your average person – for most of its history. Well, this ambiguity or confusion surrounding terms speaks to that secret history, where practice and not scholarly taxonomies or categorizations determined the shape of the world of dark psychology. Because it is shaped like this now, it is important to not smooth over the complexities it presents too much, lest you miss out on fully grasping, and perhaps taking part in, dark psychology.

That being said, look at dark persuasion and ask yourself how it could **differ** from manipulation. To start, persuasion, even of the dark variety, is much less aggressive than manipulation.

How does dark persuasion work, though? In order to answer that, first, look at the fundamentals of dark psychology. What is it? It is an intensely intimate method of control predicated on the subconscious of another person. With manipulation, there are shortcuts to accessing the subconscious of another person based on the basic nature of the human psyche. People are generally, even overwhelmingly, susceptible to at least some methods of manipulation, and those methods work even if you know very little about the person on which you are trying to use them. This is not so with dark persuasion. Dark persuasion, instead, is predicated on a certain kind of dark intimacy with your target. You have to know and understand his or her drives, interests, and dislikes. The more you know, the more effective the persuasion of your subject will be. In dark persuasion, unlike in manipulation, the dark psychology practitioner comes to understand the mind of the target in an old-fashioned way, by way of study, observation, and time spent around the target.

Note the term **dark intimacy** used above. It will come back later. For the time being, however, it warrants some unpacking. How, exactly, does dark intimacy differ from regular intimacy? The answer, as always, lies in intent. For the average person, intimacy is an end in itself. When the average person is emotionally intimate with another person, he or she feels seen, heard, appreciated, and generally good. Emotional intimacy is the bedrock upon which normal relationships, be they platonic, romantic, sexual, or familial, are based. They are always a **means** to an end. It is a necessary component of the dark psychology methodology of control.

Therefore, intimacy in the context of dark psychology, what you would call dark intimacy, could not be further from its normal, not dark counterpart. It can take many forms. Dark intimacy may be based solely on the study of its target's inner workings. From Freud, we have the insight that, with enough observation and study, the subconscious of any person can become legible to others. Freud didn't have control of the other in mind, but the principle remains the same. That is to say; dark intimacy does not necessarily imply a real relationship of any kind. That being said, it can. Another form of dark intimacy, darker still than that dark clinical intimacy, is dark intimacy developed the old-fashioned way. It comes from entering into a relationship with another person and feigning normalcy, pretending that you are in the relationship for all the normal reasons, while secretly maintaining that relationship for self-interested, anti-social ends. Only after you have established what the other person perceives as real, mutual trust will you be able to enact your dark persuasion, but it will be very effective. Once you understand the target of your dark persuasion inside and out by way of dark intimacy, you can begin.

You already know the importance of deception to all practices of dark psychology. It comes out in full force here, because what underpins the differences between dark and regular persuasion is that, unlike regular persuasion, dark persuasion has no fidelity to the truth or the world. It has fidelity only to success in persuading its target and to the whims and wishes of the person deploying it. So, once you, the dark psychology practitioner, have developed a suitably intimate, which is to say **close**, understanding of your target, such that you understand as many of his or her wishes, insecurities, drives, and desires as you can, you deploy persuasion techniques as needed without any heed to the truth. If your target wants to be beautiful, and you want your target to make a large purchase on your behalf, for instance, you may be able to find a way to convince him or her that he or she will be more physically attracted to you if he or she makes that purchase for you. When you are practicing dark persuasion, it does not matter if this could not be further from the truth. Even if you knew that never in a million years, would you find that target physically attractive?

These are the fundamental attributes of persuasion, or, more specifically, dark persuasion. The detour into dark intimacy was necessary, because without dark intimacy of some kind or another dark persuasion simply can not work. Unlike manipulation, which has a higher success rate on strangers, dark persuasion must be predicated on some knowledge of the target's inner workings, or at the very least in-depth knowledge of how and what most people desire.

Chapter 11 Solutions to Overcome Manipulation

Cutting off manipulation ties

This chapter is the climax of this book as you might be reading this chapter mainly because you have had enough of being manipulated or living with manipulative friends, family members, or your significant other. You might have reached the 'never again' point in your life after your bad experiences with manipulation. Getting long-lasting solutions to manipulation could end life's challenges and make the world a better place to live. Not every manipulative act leads to success; some lead to distress. Before solving any manipulative deeds, you need to ask yourself the following:

After being manipulated, do you feel that you have been taken advantage of?

Do you attempt to manipulate others?

What are the reasons if you ever feel like manipulating others?

Do you regret failing to be smarter once you have been manipulated?

Can someone make you do what you do not want to do?

Do you feel guilty if you fail to do what people request you to do?

Do you feel angry, frustrated, or uncomfortable when around specific people?

This is not the best time to ask why manipulators manipulate others, but it is the best time to know that they will never do it again to you.

Consider a case where you desperately need attention from your friends mainly because your parents did not give it to you during your childhood. The attention could be sought from others because maybe your partner gives you none. In this case, you will have allowed people to manipulate you. You might fall for the appraisal quotes; being told how beautiful or handsome you are, how amazing and different you are, then you get manipulated in this kind of a fix. You will feel special and feel appreciated more than another person would.

If you are a victim of this, you must have reached your final straw with such kinds of manipulators and now, you need solutions.

You should avoid being desperate – This means that after every bad experience, you should never go seeking attention immediately. You should avoid any contact with a person, especially after being hurt as they may end up taking advantage of that and keep manipulating you.

When a deal sounds and appears too good, you should not give in immediately – This can be helpful especially in resisting some marketing manipulation tactics where sales persons try to persuade you to purchase a certain product that has been given subtle qualities, praised for its goodness, and how amazing it is. You should buy what you want without getting convinced to buy what you do not want.

Learn to control yourself even in the midst of flattery. Note that too much flattery can mean manipulation underway. Whenever people flirt too much or insist on getting a certain demand granted, always stop them immediately. Even if cooperation is good, it is bad at the same time as it can rub away your way of thinking.

You need to separate the 'truly needful people' in your life from those 'claiming to be in need' kind of people. There are people who genuinely need your help and those that you feel it is your responsibility or duty to help them. Such may include your child, aging parent, or a sick person. Then there are those that want to make you feel that their problem is your problem and their responsibilities are your responsibilities and that you are supposed to solve them. To sort out between a manipulator and a truly needful person, ask a friend or relative who is objective and cool. If they say 'No,' then that should be your response, too.

Manipulators can opt to be emotional to get what they want, as described in the manipulative techniques or ways on how to identify a manipulator. You should also learn how you should deal with emotional manipulation. You should note that:

It is of no use trying to be straightforward to an emotional manipulator. This is because every statement you make is always turned down. Consider the case below:

You: I am so disappointed, you forgot my birthday!

Your friend: It really makes me feel bad that you think I would by any chance forget your birthday. I wish I told you of the stress I have right now, but I did not want to stress you, too. I guess I should have valued your birthday, I am sorry.

In this case, your friend will even shed tears when responding. You will find yourself with nothing more to say, and ending up babysitting your friend's angst. The solution to this is, trust your guts, senses, and instincts, do not take any apology or excuse that feels like nonsense.

An emotional persuader or manipulator always comes in the picture of a willing helper. Emotional manipulators will still agree to what you ask them to do for you. When you say 'Thank you,' they reply with sighs and non-verbal cues that insinuates that they do not want to help you. When you question them, they will respond angrily and say you are unreasonable. The solution to this is avoiding challenging their sighs, make them accountable for their offer to help out. Leave them to help and walk away to avoid these crazy dramas.

Do not entertain them

In your relationships, you should never question your sanity or keep records for what was said or promised. A manipulator will turn things around and justify that they never gave any promises. These manipulators lie a lot so that can make you even doubt your senses. Carry a notebook and start making notes after every conversation, claiming that you feel you are so forgetful and that they should not be worried about your craziness. This helps you remove yourself from their range and avoid manipulation.

When conditioned to act necessarily to decrease your guilty feelings, be on-the-know that you are getting manipulated. Manipulators make you feel guilty for almost everything; too much caring, loving, emotional, nurture, or support enough. Once you do anything for them, they never appreciate it and can even tell you that they did not expect whatever you did for them. You need to stop fighting other people's battles. Have a line to say to the manipulators who make you feel guilty. Tell them, 'I have great confidence to do this, do it your own'. Sit back and listen to their response; they probably lack one.

You should avoid people who cannot talk to you or deal with issues directly. They always let you know everything through their friends; they literally tend to send people to tell you what they want. Scream at them and never entertain any connections they send you.

When manipulators are angry, they tend to influence the environment and want everyone else to feel like them. They want to make people do things their way, by getting angry with everyone and expecting everyone to respond friendly. Remember, you also have your own psychological strains and needs, do not give in to such nonsense.

Anyone who is not accountable for their mess, no responsibility, and always complains about what other people do to them, is the kind of manipulators you should avoid with an immediate effect. You should never apologize for a mess that you are not responsible for. Leave the manipulator to realize their own mistakes and apologize appropriately. Avoid contact with the would-be manipulators. Just listen to them but act differently. They cannot hold you and force you to get manipulated anyway.

Setting personal boundaries can also be a long-lasting solution to manipulation. Before your relationship goes too far, and before anyone learns you in and out, set limits, then having to change in the midway. You can do so by stating the kind of behaviors you like or dislike. For instance, tell them they should not call you any time they feel like, mostly past 9 pm. Clearly define your goals so that it will be possible to know when you are getting manipulated. When you know your direction, it would be complicated for someone to influence you.

Be responsible and keep track of what you say or do. This helps you avoid getting blamed for other people's mistakes. Keep your notebook or computers safe from anybody else at work, school, or at home. People can access your information and defend themselves with it when they are accusing you.

Do not be emotional in every occasion. Your manipulators are waiting for this moment. They can easily manipulate you when you are emotionally down. Manipulators know how to twist the situation until they control you.

Differentiate manipulation from mental illness. Sounds funny, right? It can be a serious case, especially when manipulation becomes an everyday action. A manipulator cannot be independent, responsible, or accountable. Some of these conditions need proper treatment.

The truth hurts! Always hit any manipulator with the truth. Make their friends your enemies as this destroys their power base. By doing this, you will be a unique person that no one would want to mess around with.

Manipulation does not always entail other people manipulating you. You can as well be a manipulator, and hence, you need solutions on how to stop being a manipulator. Ask yourself whether you are a psychopath, a narcissist, aggressive, and any other characteristics of a manipulator. If you are not egotistical or you do not do anything centered at your own interests, then you are not a manipulator.

Take time to know what you want

Appreciate the honesty and avoid resenting people

Learn to let go anything you cannot have; it is not the end of the world.

Do not act out of defensiveness just because people turned down your requests. Embrace every response you get.

Do not take everything too personal since this makes you feel powerless and end up manipulating others.

Manipulative people in society are meant to be ignored. Never correct them as this pulls you into their trap. You should know that guilt is a senseless emotion and that manipulators can make you feel the guilt of your mistakes or past. Do not compromise them. Stop doubting yourself and live your life appropriately. You need to feel good about yourself, be confident, and always be happy about your achievements. Appreciate and believe in what you are doing.

Conclusion

The best part is unlike intelligence quotient, the emotional quotient can be developed through regular practice, training, and application. Improving your emotional intelligence is a continuous and dynamic process that only helps you enhance your skills with time.

I expect this book was able to teach you how to master your emotions and to improve your communication skills. Hopefully, this book was able to build up your confidence and make you a stronger person. I hope this book was able to give you insight into the concept and meaning of emotional intelligence, and now you feel confident in your abilities and are able to succeed.

I hope this book was able to help you develop and improve your communication skills. I hope this book was able to help you develop emotional intelligence and better understand the concept of it. Hopefully, the examples in the book were helpful, useful, and easy to use. I hope this book helped you feel more in control and happier in the long run. I hope this book was able to prepare you for the next step in the journey.

Developing Dark Psychology skills is a very challenging but rewarding work out. It is important to invest in building strong romantic relationships by constantly nurturing your self-awareness, self-management, and social recognition skills. This will open you up to a greater relationship with yourself and others in which you will come to a point of full understanding. Learning how exactly to do this and placing it into practice may be harder for a few than others however the important key to remember is that it is an art that exists within all of us.

Emotions are one of the major the different parts of being human, therefore the further we can understand our very own emotions the easier it all becomes to relate to others whether we agree with how they feel or not. Strengthening these abilities could be of great help in all conditions and interactions and the glad tidings are that you can learn these abilities at any age or stage in your daily life to propel you to greatness!

If you want to persuade people, you have to be ready to make people see and feel like it was their decision.

Many people want to manipulate others for short-term gain. However, the genuine art of manipulation is defined by the long game. One has to be patient. The same way professionals make their skills look easy; you need to make manipulation sound easy. But it will take time and patience to learn to execute the manipulation secrets.

One thing about the manipulation that you need to keep in mind is that you should never reveal your true intentions. Maintain your consciousness of how you are making them feel and attempt to manipulate for the best.

The next step is to practice! Use those examples and make them your own. If you never try then nothing will ever change. You need to try, take that first step and be prepared for the solution. Mastering your emotions can be a challenge, but I know you can succeed. I believe in you. You will be successful and feel more accomplished. You will become more observant, appreciative and stress-free.

CHAPTER BONUS

What's Dark Psychology

Before we take a look at some of the methods that come with dark psychology and how it can be used against you, it is important to know exactly what this form of psychology is about. Psychology, or an understanding of how the human mind works, is a part of all of our lives. Psychology is going to underpin everything in our lives from advertising to finance, crime to religion, and even from hate to love. Someone who is able to understand these psychological principles is someone who really holds onto the key to human influence.

This is not an easy task, which is why most people don't possess it. Learning all of the different principles of psychology is not necessary. Start with the lessons in these pages and you'll have a solid foundation. You have to be able to read people, understand what makes them tick, and understand why they may react in ways that may not be normally expected. And even then, you may need to spend time taking classes and reading through countless books to gain a complete understanding. It depends how far you want to go with this.

So, if only a few people really understand psychology and how the human mind works, why is it so important to know what this is? It is because those who do know what it is and how to use it can choose to use that power and that knowledge against you.

How Is Dark Psychology Used Today?

While some people are going to use these dark psychology tactics in order to harm their victim, there are times when you may use these tactics without the intent of negatively manipulating another person. Some of these tactics were either unintentionally or intentionally added to our toolbox from a variety of means that could include:

• When you were a child, you would see how adults, especially those close to you, behaved.

• When you were a teenager, the mind and your ability to truly understand the behaviors around you were expanded.

• You were able to watch others use the tactics and then succeed.

• Using the tactics may have been unintentional in the beginning, but when you found that it worked to get you what you wanted, you would start to use those tactics in an intentional manner.

• Some people, such as a politician, a public speaker, or a salesperson, would be trained to use these types of tactics to get what they want.

Dark Psychology Tactics That Are Used on a Regular Basis

- Love flooding: This would include any buttering up, praising, or complimenting people to get them to comply with the request that you want. If you want someone to help you move some items into your home, you may use love flooding in order to make them feel good, which could make it more likely that they will help you. A dark manipulator could also use it to make the other person feel attached to them and then get them to do things that they may not normally do.

- Lying: This would include telling the victim an untrue version of the situation. It can also include a partial truth or exaggerations with the goal of getting what you wanted done.

- Love denial: This one can be hard on the victim because it can make them feel lost and abandoned by the manipulator. This one basically includes withholding affection and love until you are able to get what you want out of the victim.

- Withdrawal: This would be when the victim is given the silent treatment or is avoided until they meet the needs of the other person.

- Restricting choices: The manipulator may give their victim access to some choices, but they do this in order to distract them from the choices that they don't want the victim to make.

- Semantic manipulation: This is a technique where the manipulator is going to use some commonly known words, ones that have accepted meanings by both parties, in a conversation. But then they will tell the victim, later on, that they had meant something completely different when they used that word. The new meaning is often going to change up the entire definition and could make it so that the conversation goes the way the manipulator wanted, even though the victim was tricked.

• Reverse psychology: This is when you tell someone to do something in one manner, knowing that they will do the opposite. But the opposite action is what the manipulator wanted to happen in the first place.

Who Will Deliberately Use Dark Tactics?

There are many different people who may choose to use these dark tactics against you. They can be found in many different aspects of your life, which is why it is so important to learn how to stay away from them. Some of the people who are able to use some of these dark psychology tactics deliberately include:

• Narcissists: These individuals are going to have a bloated sense of their own self-worth, and they will have the need to make others believe that they are superior as well. In order to meet their desires of being worshipped and adored by everyone they meet, they will use persuasion and dark psychology.

• Sociopaths: Those who are sociopaths are charming, intelligent, and persuasive. But they only act this way to get what they want. They lack any emotions and they are not able to feel any remorse. This means that they have no issue with using the tactics of dark psychology to get what they want, including taking it as far as creating superficial relationships.

- Politicians: With the help of dark psychology, a politician could convince someone to cast votes for them simply by convincing these people that their point of view is the right one.

- Salespeople: Not all salespeople are going to use dark tactics against you. But it is possible that some, especially those who are really into getting their sales numbers and being the best, will not think twice about using dark persuasion in order to manipulate people.

- Leaders: Throughout history, there have been plenty of leaders who will use the techniques of dark psychology in order to get their team members, subordinates, and citizens do what they want.

- Selfish people: This could be any person that you come across who will make sure that their own needs are put before anyone else's. They aren't concerned about others, and they will let others forego their benefits so that they can benefit. If the situation benefits them, it is fine if it benefits someone else. But if someone is going to be the loser, it will be the other person and not them.

This list is important because it is going to serve two purposes. First, it is going to help you be more aware of the people who may try to manipulate you to do things that you don't want to do, and it can be there to help out with self-realization. Being on the lookout for those who want to get something out of you, without any concerns about how it will affect you, is one of the main goals of this book so that you can arm yourself against dark psychology.

The term "mental manipulation" is often thrown around on social media and in mainstream communications. In fact, it is quite common to hear this expression used in reference to large public events, political campaigning and advertising. The fact of the matter is that most folks have a general understanding of what it refers to but may not be clear on the specific of what this term encompasses.

In short, mental manipulation is controlling and twisting a person's state of mind to make them want to do what you want to be done. A manipulator influences the will of others through the use deception or underhand techniques.

As such, manipulation implies a degree of force upon targets, that is, the manipulator will try their best to force their targets to do what they will, especially if the targets do not wish to comply.

Now, I am not talking about kidnapping folks and brainwashing them like it is done in the movies. I am talking about subtle techniques and strategies which are used to get others to go along without them actually realizing they are being manipulated.

As a matter of fact, the best manipulators make it seem like people are doing things of their own accord rather than acting upon the provocation of some external force. Nevertheless, there is a degree of forces that goes along with manipulation. For example, television stations will force you to watch their programming and advertising in order to get you to purchase the products and services of their sponsor's.

However, the coercion shown in this case is quite simple to get around: you can just change the channel. Yet, programming and advertising is designed in such a way that you won't want to change channel.

Other types of manipulation can be a lot more overt. For instance, political parties and candidates will promote themselves by littering their campaigns with calls to action such as "vote for the best candidate" or "vote for so-and-so if you value your children's future". These calls to action are blatant attempts at swaying voters' opinions.

That is why the first part of this book is dedicated to understanding and identifying manipulation as it is commonly practiced. I am not talking about some dark cabal that is trying to secretly rule the world through controlling the minds of every single human on this planet. In fact, I am referring to the ways in which trained individuals will attempt to influence your opinion to get you to go along with their agenda.

When you uncover their techniques, you will not only be able to protect yourself, and your loved ones, from these influences, you will be also be able to get your own agenda across. While I am not asking you to openly go out there and control the minds of those with whom you come into contact, I am asking you to use these techniques to help you get ahead when you need that extra nudge.

So, sit back because we are going on quite a ride.

EXTRACT FROM:

"Dark Psychology Secrets:
How To Influence People To Positive Behavior In Relationship
With Nlp. Discover The Art Of Reading And Analyze People,
Learning Emotional Manipulation And Mind Control."

Made in the USA
Monee, IL
03 February 2021